How to Catalog a Rare Book

How to Catalog a Rare Book

Second edition, revised

Paul Shaner Dunkin

AMERICAN LIBRARY ASSOCIATION
Chicago 1973

Library of Congress Cataloging in Publication Data

Dunkin, Paul Shaner, 1905–
How to catalog a rare book.

Includes bibliographies.
1. Cataloging of rare books. I. Title.
Z695.74.D8 1973 025.3'41 72-6515
ISBN 0-8389-0141-7

Printed in the United States of America
Second Printing, September 1973

To the Memory of EDWIN ELIOTT WILLOUGHBY

Contents

Illustrations

Preface to the Second Edition

A new edition of this book seems necessary for at least two reasons: collation formula and title transcription.

While I was writing the first edition of *How to Catalog a Rare Book,* Fredson Bowers' *Principles of Bibliographical Description* (1949) was published. In it Bowers endorsed a highly complicated collation formula to be used in printed bibliographies and in papers in bibliographical journals. I set forth in my book a much simpler collation formula for cataloging, and I still believe that it is practical.

Meanwhile, somewhat to my surprise, many compilers of printed bibliographies and authors of papers in bibliographical journals have used the Bowers formula or some version of it. Although catalogers will never (I hope) use the Bowers formula in their entries, they may often have to compare a book in hand with a Bowers-formula description in some printed bibliography or bibliographical journal. This new edition of my book tries to make the Bowers formula easy for catalogers to understand.

Since writing the book, I have spent ten more years at the Folger Library and twelve years at Rutgers University Graduate School of Library Service, teaching courses in cataloging and analytical bibliography. These experiences have convinced me that a briefer and simpler title transcription than I had advocated in my book is quite enough. In this second edition the original treatment of transcription is again given, but a simpler treatment, also described, is probably a better choice.

1. Whys and Wherefores

Anything written on rare-book cataloging is bound to be controversial. Some catalogers have finally discovered that for most books brief and simple cataloging is enough. An adequate catalog card for any book tells where to find that book and why anyone might want to find it. People want to find an ordinary book because they want to read it. Simplified cataloging serves well enough for such a book because it gives a call number and tells what the book is about.

But people want to find a rare book because they want to look at it. The rare book is a fascinating material object, a document in the history of civilization. If people want only to read it, a microfilm or a reprint will do, and the cataloging of that microfilm or reprint should, of course, be as brief and simple as the cataloging of any ordinary book. But the fact that the rare book itself is valued as a material object must be the keynote of any useful approach to rare-book cataloging. An adequate catalog card for a rare book will tell enough about physical makeup to set that book apart from all other books.

How much is enough? Probably no two catalogers will agree. I have stated my preferences and tried to defend them. But in each case I have tried also to describe rejected practices in enough detail to help those catalogers who may wish to use them or may find them used in bibliographies they consult. I hope, however, that I have made it clear that adequate description of a book as a material object always means, first, more attention to title transcription than in the case of ordinary books and, second, collation by gatherings as well as by pages.

Illustrations of the problems to be faced have been drawn largely from English and American books printed by the handpress. Citations in foreign languages might have made reading somewhat more difficult, and irregularities in physical makeup are much more frequent in books printed a sheet at a time on the handpress than in books printed on the modern machine. Finally, every printed book, no matter where or when produced, is basically much the same: it is made up of one or more gatherings, each of which results from printing and then folding into leaves one large sheet of paper, part of one sheet, or more than one sheet. Therefore, description of any rare book follows the same general lines. A cancel leaf, for instance, serves the same purpose and is described in the same way whether it appears in a Dutch incunabulum or in an American best seller of today.

I have not attempted to define "rare book." It would take a thick treatise to do just that. In any event, it is not the cataloger's job to decide if a book is rare; that has been decided before the book reaches his desk. For his purposes any book which has value primarily as a physical object is a rare book.

I have written only of cataloging problems peculiar to rare books. A rare book, like any other book, requires careful establishment of its author entry, added entries, and subject headings. All of these standard cataloging practices, however, are described in the American Library Association and Library of Congress rules and in other books; there is no need to repeat them here.

It is true that the type of cataloging I have described is seldom done. But there would be no reason for writing this book if it were quite generally done and everyone knew how to do it. Rare books are seldom adequately cataloged, simply because few people know how easy it is to catalog them and how helpful good cards for them can be. Good cards are helpful not only in a local catalog but also in a union catalog, because the potential users of information about a rare book are everywhere.

So I have written, first of all, for general catalogers in college and public libraries. Every such library has at least a few rare books, and any general cataloger can make useful cards for them. I have tried to tell what to look for in a rare book and to insist that what is found can be described briefly in everyday language. At the same time, catalogers of large rare-book collections, students of English and American literature, students of descriptive bibliography, and, indeed, anyone at all interested in rare books may find some use for what I have written. Some sections—for instance, the chapter on format—contain suggestions and information which, I believe, had never appeared in print before the first edition of this book (1951).

Finally, I have written primarily of entry in a card catalog, but I have tried to note differences which entry in a book catalog or printed bibliography might involve. More and more, printed catalogs of rare-book collections are being made available to the general public.

Cataloging rare books, of course, takes more time and money than ordinary cataloging. Moreover, some rare books are not particularly expensive, and adequate cataloging may cost more than the books themselves. Because a rare book is of value primarily as a physical object, the library will want to examine this object just as carefully as it would examine any other physical object it might acquire—e.g., a desk for the director's office. Some people feel that entry for the rare book in the catalog need be only skeletal and that details of the cataloger's examination of the book—e.g., collation by gatherings—to find out if the book is complete and exactly what it was said to be by the dealer or the donor can be kept in a private file. There is, indeed, some saving here, but it is only the saving of clerical time needed to record the cataloger's professional findings, which may be of considerable help to the user of the catalog. If a library feels it cannot afford to catalog rare books adequately, perhaps it cannot afford to acquire them. No administrator would think of building a twenty-room library, or even accepting one as a gift, if his community could efficiently use only five rooms and could not afford the upkeep of twenty.

When a library acquires a book, it acquires also the obligation to share that book as effectively as possible. This obligation is greater if the book is a rare book, because a rare book, unlike other books, cannot be bought by just anyone who happens to want it and has the cash to buy it. Also, the people who want it may live anywhere in the world, not just in the library's community. Now, books can be shared adequately only if they are cataloged adequately. The library which sticks rare books into a showcase and refuses to put useful entries for them into both its own catalog and a union catalog is no better than the wealthy collector who hides his books away in a vault where he and a few friends can gloat over them.

2. A Few Books about Books

In no sense does this list pretend to be complete; it is only what I call it. The books listed here are basic books or examples of basic kinds of books. Arrangement under each topic is alphabetical by authors' surnames. Future reference to these books will be only by author and page number.

Bibliography

Rare-book cataloging, like all cataloging, is only a division of bibliography, and some books on bibliography in general have much to help the cataloger of rare books.

Esdaile, Arundell. *Esdaile's Manual of Bibliography.* rev. ed. by Roy Stokes. New York: Barnes & Noble, 1967.

A brief statement of much basic information with useful reading lists.

McKerrow, Ronald B. *An Introduction to Bibliography for Literary Students.* Oxford: Clarendon Pr., 1927.

This is a book which the cataloger will want to read through several times and to keep on his desk. It is concise, lucid, and literate. Over forty years of intensive research have brought to light remarkably little essential information which McKerrow did not present, or at least anticipate, in his masterly work.

Book Production

Bühler, Curt F. *The Fifteenth Century Book: The Scribes, the Printers, the Decorators.* Philadelphia: Univ. of Pennsylvania Pr., 1960.

This is an informative, thoughtful, well-printed book.

Carter, John. *ABC for Book-Collectors.* New York: Alfred A. Knopf, 1952.

This little book has gone through several editions, each of them witty and wise. The technical terms of the book collector are the technical terms of the rare-book cataloger, and they are all briefly and accurately defined here.

Library of Congress. *Papermaking, Art and Craft: An Account Derived from the Exhibition Presented in the Library of Congress . . . Opened on April 21, 1968.* Washington: The Library, 1968.

This attractively printed and illustrated pamphlet is a useful brief history.

Moxon, Joseph. *Mechanick Exercises on the Whole Art of Printing (1683–4)* . . . . , ed. by Herbert Davis and Harry Carter. 2d ed. London: Oxford Univ. Pr., 1962.

Moxon's was the earliest printers' manual, and for almost two centuries manuals both in England and in America showed its influence. This scholarly modern edition with its notes and illustrations may help the reader to understand the making of a printed book, both now and in Moxon's day.

Silver, Rollo G. *The American Printer 1787–1825.* Charlottesville: Univ. Pr. of Virginia, 1967.

McKerrow deals largely with English books; this and Wroth's book, in the following note, supplement McKerrow with an excellent approach to the understanding of books printed in America. The reader may find Silver's and Wroth's description of the handpress easier to understand than McKerrow's. Both books are attractively printed and illustrated.

Wroth, Lawrence C. *The Colonial Printer.* Portland, Maine: Southworth-Anthoensen Pr., 1938.

Book Description

McKerrow, Esdaile, and several other books on bibliography in general have sections on book description; the following items are devoted largely or entirely to description alone.

American Library Association. *Anglo-American Cataloging Rules. North American Text.* Chicago: The Association, 1967.

The sections on description in this and the British text, like earlier editions of the ALA rules, have much that is applicable to rare books but also much that seems not to face the problems appropriately.

Bowers, Fredson. *Principles of Bibliographical Description.* Princeton: Princeton Univ. Pr., 1949.

Based on Greg (see note on Greg below) and, to some extent, McKerrow, this elaborate and arbitrary codification has to some extent dominated description in printed bibliographies.

Cowley, J. D. *Bibliographical Description and Cataloguing.* London: Grafton, 1949.

This book owes much to the principles set forth by Greg, and it deals primarily with the preparation of printed bibliographies, but it has a well-annotated list of reference works.

Foxon, David F. *Thoughts on the History and Future of Bibliographical Description.* Los Angeles and Berkeley: Univ. of California Pr., 1970.

A thought-provoking antidote to the Greg-Bowers excesses.

Greg, W. W. "A Formulary of Collation," *The Library,* 4th series, 14: 365–82 (1934).

This, of course, is not a book, and it was superseded by Greg's discussion in the fourth volume of his bibliography of early English printed drama listed below. The article is included here because it marks the beginning of the emphasis on elaborate detail so fully stated by Bowers.

Library of Congress. *Studies of Descriptive Cataloging.* Washington: Govt. Print. Off., 1946. Referred to as LC *Studies.*

Although concerned with description of books in general, this book has profound implications for the elaborate description of rare books.

Standards of Bibliographical Description by Curt F. Bühler, James G. McManaway, Lawrence C. Wroth. Philadelphia: Univ. of Pennsylvania Pr., 1949.

Dealing with incunabula, early English literature, and early Americana, respectively, the contributors show no little diversity of "standards."

Stevenson, Allan. *A Bibliographical Method for the Description of Botanical Books.* (Reprinted from *Catalogue of Botanical Books in the Collection of Rachel McMasters Miller Hunt,* 1961.)

This pamphlet adapts and extends the Greg-Bowers system to the description of works with plates issued in parts, in folio, or in broadsheet.

Serials

The cataloger needs a speaking acquaintance, if not more, with at least these three serials:

The Library. (Transactions of The Bibliographical Society.) Quarterly.

The Papers of the Bibliographical Society of America. Quarterly.

Studies in Bibliography; Papers of the Bibliographical Society of the University of Virginia. Annual.

Printed Bibliographies

A printed bibliography reflects its author's thinking about the description of rare books. The cataloger will, therefore, want to look carefully through a number of printed bibliographies, books like the following:

Currier, Thomas Franklin. *A Bibliography of Oliver Wendell Holmes . . . Edited by Eleanor M. Tilton.* New York and London: New York Univ. Pr., 1953.

Greg, W. W. *A Bibliography of the English Printed Drama to the Restoration.* London: Printed for the Bibliographical Soc. at the Univ. Pr., Oxford, 1939–59. 4v.

MacDonald, Hugh, and Hargreaves, Mary. *Thomas Hobbes; a Bibliography.* London: The Bibliographical Soc., 1952.

Madan, Francis F. *A New Bibliography of the Eikon Basilike of King Charles the First.* Oxford: Oxford Univ. Pr., 1950.

Russo, Dorothy Ritter. *A Bibliography of George Ade.* Indianapolis: Indiana Historical Soc., 1947.

Smith, William C., and Humphries, Charles. *A Bibliography of the Musical Works Published by the Firm of John Walsh During the Years 1721–1766.* London: The Bibliographical Soc., 1968.

3. Distinctions: Editions, Issues, Printings

If every book were exactly like every other book, or even if every edition of a book were exactly like every other edition of that book, there would be few rare books. This, of course, is not the case. Shakespeare's poems and plays in one volume differ both in appearance and in content from a Wodehouse novel. On the other hand, the Shakespeare first folio of 1623 differs almost as greatly from the collection of the great bard's works with notes and illustrations through which the student plows in college.

Editions

Apart from changes in paper and an editor's revisions of content, two editions of the same book differ chiefly, if not only, in their printing. The two editions were printed from different settings of type, and no two settings of type can ever be exactly the same.

Type may vary a great deal in the size and shape of individual letters, and when those letters are grouped into words and sentences and paragraphs, the pages of one edition may not look at all like those of another. Two editions may be printed from settings of type with identical size and style and with the same page arrangement, but even in such a case there will generally be slight differences: smaller spaces between the words in some lines, a different last word in a line now and then, a worn letter used where a sound letter appears in the other edition, and so on. Only in the (fortunately) rare case in which the printer fraudulently intends to convince people that his edition is actually another edition will he find it worth his trouble to try to prevent all easily noticed differences.

An edition, then, consists of all copies of a book printed

from a single setting of type. Ideally all copies of an edition should be identical. Actually they seldom are.

Corrections at Press

For one thing, there are corrections at press.

Suppose the book in a cataloger's hands is *Sixty Sermons Sauing Sinners' Sicke Soules,* written by his College's Founder back in England some three hundred years ago and recently presented to the library by a distinguished alumnus. The Founder's book, like all other books, is physically a group of gatherings of leaves, and each gathering was produced by printing and then folding one or more times a part of a large sheet of paper, a whole sheet, or more than one sheet. Now, while the first side of the first sheet was being printed, the reverend author himself may have dropped into the shop to scan with pardonable pride this very first part of the very first offspring of his muse. Imagine his horror if he found that in line 2 of page 3 the Reverend Dr. Heggsby, who had just been appointed Bishop of Crough, was referred to as "Hoggsty." The Founder would shriek, the press work would be stopped at once, there would be explanations and perhaps (but only perhaps, for after all the Founder's handwriting may have left much to be desired and his book would not necessarily bring heavy sales) apologies profuse. The offending letters would be corrected in all copies of the sheet printed after the Founder's shocking discovery. However, because the Founder was not (at that time and to that printer at least) an important man and because paper and printing are expensive, the printer would (perhaps privately) decide to use the uncorrected sheets also.

After all copies of the sheet had been printed on one side, they would be turned over and printed on the other side. (This is called "perfecting" the sheet.) The Founder would naturally be suspicious of all printers, and he would probably come snooping around that day also, to find that in line 10 of page 8 "Trinity" was spelled with two n's, and talk the printer into stopping work again to correct that word too. It is, of course, unlikely that the "Trinnity" error would be corrected on the very same copy of that sheet as "Hoggsty." So a copy of the first edition of the Founder's *Sermons* might have any one of the following readings:

1. "Hoggsty" on page 3 and "Trinnity" on page 8
2. "Hoggsty" on page 3 and "Trinity" on page 8, or "Heggsby" on page 3 and "Trinnity" on page 8
3. "Heggsby" on page 3 and "Trinity" on page 8.

Number 1 readings would, of course, indicate the first copies of the first sheet to be printed. But books containing these readings could not be labeled the very first copies printed. The Founder's (and the press corrector's) alert eye would no doubt catch other errors in other sheets as they were being printed, and each time the press work would stop while they also were corrected. But when the printed sheets were folded into gatherings and the gatherings collected into books, there would be no reason whatever for trying to make one group of books consist only of the number 1 copies of each sheet, another only of number 2 copies, and a third only of number 3 copies. In fact, it could not be done even if one were to try, because the number of errors discovered and the time of their discovery would vary with each side of each sheet; and no other sheet in the *Sermons* would have a sequence of corrections precisely like that of the first.

Generally speaking, all copies of a book printed from the same setting of type with variants only such as these may be safely called the same edition, and the cataloger may never have to face the problem anyway unless he catalogs many copies of the same book. At the same time, it is always worthwhile to note an error or a correction if one comes across it, and in the case of a modern book a correction may have some importance, as we shall see.

Issues

Suppose that the Founder persuaded the printer to correct the "Hoggsty" sheets already printed. This would be done by printing a single leaf (page 3 on one side, which we call the "recto," page 4 on the other, which we call the "verso") with the correct reading "Heggsby." Then, when the uncorrected copies of the first sheet were folded into a gathering, the offending "Hoggsty" leaf would be cut away and the correct leaf put in its place. The leaf removed is called a "cancelland," and the leaf which replaces it is called a "cancel."

A copy of the first edition of the *Sermons,* then, might have the leaf containing pages 3 and 4 printed correctly and folded as part of the sheet with which it belonged, or it might have this leaf printed as a detached piece of paper and pasted into place. Each of these variants would be called an "issue" of the first edition of the *Sermons.*

A cancel, however, is not the only thing which can produce an issue. The Founder might have come in a month later with another sermon and had it printed and bound with the unsold copies of the *Sermons.* Or the book might have been handled by two booksellers, each of whom insisted that the title page name him alone, and the printer could have produced the book with special title pages to please each of them. When the publisher's case binding came into vogue in the 1820s, another element was introduced; two issues of a nineteenth century book may differ only in their binding. And so on.

The question of priority of issues and even of editions is at times extremely difficult. Many catalogers blithely note on their cards "First edition, first issue" for no reason at all other than the intuitive feeling that it must be so or because they have seen the book so described in an auction catalog. The very first person who looks at that card may have in his hand a volume which is obviously an earlier issue. Life will be happier if the book is described thoroughly without using "First edition" or "First issue," unless some good printed bibliography can be cited on the card.

An issue, then, does not involve a major change in the setting of type. It uses the original printed leaves of an edition, but with some important alteration. An edition may consist of any number of issues.

Printings

The printer of an early book had a limited supply of type, and he seldom left type standing after he had used it to print one side of a sheet. Instead, he returned it to the case so that he could use it in setting copy for a later sheet. But with the invention of modern stereotype and electrotype plates, it became possible to reprint an entire book many times from what amounts to the same setting of type.

Each reprinting, of course, offers a chance to make small corrections in the plates, but at the same time individual letters may be wearing badly and even breaking in some places. These corrections would be different from those made in the Founder's *Sermons* because they would be found in all copies of the reprinting.

Often a reprinting is noted on the verso of the title page—e.g., "Second printing" or "Reprinted July 1930." In books like Joseph Thomas' *Universal Pronouncing Dictionary of Biography and Mythology* the worn type of the old plates contrasts vividly with the fresh type of the inserted revisions.

There is some tendency to consider each reprinting a new edition. Each reprinting may, indeed, represent a new and distinct publishing venture. But it is often hard to tell one printing from another and, in any event, the setting of type remains largely if not entirely the same.

The original printing as well as each reprinting from the same setting of type (or from plates made from that type) may be called an "impression" or simply a "printing." Probably "printing" is the better term because "impression" has often been used, particularly on the title pages of early books, to mean "edition."

Photographic Reprints

Technically the photographic reprint of a book is not a new edition, because it is not from a new setting of type;

it is not a printing, because it is not printed from the same setting of type; and it is not an issue, even though new prefatory or other material may have been added to it. It is not even a rare book; it may take one of several forms—e.g., photostat, microform, printed book. But it will probably be most used if it is listed in the catalog alongside the version of the book it reproduces.

Distinctions: Cataloger and Bibliographer

"Edition," "issue," "printing": the conventional view of these distinctions has long been that they should be based on easily recognized physical differences among the variant forms in which the same book may appear, and that strict uniformity in their definition does not greatly matter. Catalogers share this conventional view.

Some bibliographers, however, use also an intermediate term "state," and they feel that the history of the printing of a particular variant, rather than its physical characteristics, should decide its classification as edition, issue, or state. Further, they urge that strict uniformity in definition is necessary for reference purposes and as a help to further bibliographical study of the variant.

The chief difficulty with definitions based on the printing history of the book is that they are hard to apply. Bowers, for instance, fills over a hundred pages with detailed discussion and intricate distinctions. Any one of five conditions may result in a variant state; any one of three in a reissue; any one of another three in a separate issue; and any one of four in an edition. Many of these fifteen conditions are subdivided; the first has five subclasses.

All this would not be so bad if each class and subclass were sharply separated and readily recognizable and if there were no more classes than Bowers describes. This, of course, is not the case. The history of the printing of any book differs from that of any other book and may easily involve situations not considered even in Bowers' lengthy discussion; indeed, he professes to list only the major classes.

Uniformity also raises questions. With regard to reference purposes, we cannot use the word "issue" (for instance) alone even if we follow Bowers' definition; instead, we say "issue with cancel title leaf" or the like—i.e., we add the *element of variation,* and, once we have done that, it matters not at all what we have called it in the first place. With regard to purposes of further study, we may not use the word "issue" until we know the complete history of the book, and no further bibliographical study is then needed. This is shown dramatically in Greg's correction in his *Bibliography of the English Printed Drama,* item 279 (a), because further study by another scholar proved "that there are not two issues of the edition, but merely two states" (vol.4, p.1679).

The plain fact, of course, is that an infinitely greater number of books are listed in catalogs than are described in bibliographies. As a result, there is more need for reference between catalogs and other catalogs or between catalogs and bibliographies than between bibliographies and other bibliographies. This will be possible only if definitions reflect traditional distinctions based on easily recognized physical differences between variants.

Distinctions: Conclusion

Books, then, differ from one another because they are different works or because they are different editions, issues, printings, or photographic reprints of the same work. An "edition" consists of all copies of a book printed from the same setting of type. A "printing" consists of all copies printed at the same time from the same setting of type; for most books printed before 1800 and for many printed since then, edition and printing are the same, because the type was not left standing after it had once been used. An "issue" results when some important change is made in the book but the setting of type remains fundamentally the same. An edition may consist of any number of printings, and each printing may consist of any number of issues.

These distinctions are neither pedantic nor academic. How often someone thought it worthwhile to put a particular piece of writing into print so that it could be read by many people, and what happened to words and phrases during the printing, make up a significant chapter in the history of a book and its influences on our life and thought.

4. On Opening the Book: Title-Page Transcription

A book's title page is like a man's face. More eloquently than any other single part of the body, the face tells what the man is like and how he differs from other men. In like manner, the title page generally sets a book apart from most other books.

Broadly speaking, there are four approaches to transcription: (1) quasi-facsimile, (2) full content only, (3) calculated risk, and (4) photographic reproduction. We shall look at each in some detail.

Quasi-Facsimile

It has become conventional, particularly in printed bibliographies, for a transcription of a title page to reproduce as nearly as possible the kinds of type used, contracted forms, ligatures, line endings, punctuation, small ornaments and so on. This is called "quasi-facsimile transcription," and it has been elaborately developed in such scholarly works as Greg's bibliography of early printed English plays and Dorothy Russo's bibliography of George Ade.

Bibliographers differ in details of quasi-facsimile transcription. There are excellent statements by Greg (*Bibl.* vol.4, p.cxxxv–cxlviii) and by Bowers (p.135–80).

Different kinds of type cannot be reproduced on a typed catalog card, but they can be indicated readily enough. Underlining will do for italic, and a row of dots beneath words can represent black letter. A few alterations in the keyboard will provide unusual letters and symbols. The title page illustrated in figure 1 might be transcribed thus:

¶ THE NEW found vvorlde, or *Antarctike, wherin is contained* wõderful and strange **things, as well of humaine treatures,** *as Beastes, Fishes, Foules, and Serpents,* **Trees, Plants, Mines of** Golde and Siluer: garnished with **many learned authorities,** trauailed and written in the French tong, by that excellent learned man, master ANDREVVE THEVET. And now newly translated into Englishe, wherein is reformed the errours of the auncient Cosmographers.

¶ *Imprinted at London, by Henrie Bynneman, for* Thomas Hacket. And are to be sold at his shop in Poules Church-yard, at the signe of the Key.

FIG. 1. A title page. Reproduced, with permission of the Folger Shakespeare Library, Washington, D.C.

¶ THE NEW/ found vvorlde, or/ Antarctike, wherin is contai-/ned wõderful and ſtrange/ things, as well of humaine crea-/ tures, as Beaſtes, Fiſhes, Foules, and Ser-/ pents, Trees, Plants, Mines of/ Golde and Siluer: garnished with/ many learned aucthorities,/ trauailed and written in the French/ tong, by that excellent learned/ man, maſter **ANDREVVE/ THEVET.**/ And now newly tranſlated into Engliſhe, / wherein is reformed the errours of/ the auncient Coſmo-/ graphers./ ¶ Imprinted at London,/ by Henrie Bynneman, for / Thomas Hacket./ And are to be ſold at his ſhop in Poules Church-/yard, at the ſigne of the Key.

This typed representation is quite as useful as a printed quasi-facsimile transcription. The actual typing is no more difficult and no more time-consuming than is any typing in which accuracy is essential. Of course, even the quasi-facsimile transcription cannot tell everything. For instance, Thevet's name is in much smaller type than are the first two words of the title, and the space between the seventeenth and the eighteenth lines is much greater than that between any other two consecutive lines on the page. A word or line printed in red would be hard to show. An engraved title page (such as that shown in fig. 2) has features different from the title set in type—e.g., the long tail of Q (fig. 2, line 6). Ligatures could be represented only by drawing them in. Such fine points, however, may often be of little importance.

Indeed, some features of the title page which the quasi-facsimile transcription does preserve are seldom needed. The portraits attached to a post-office bulletin board each represent the usual assortment of eyes, ears, nose and mouth, but only one of them reveals a worthy with an Andy Gump chin, a scar on his right cheek, and a wart on his nose. Anyone at all familiar with Elizabethan title pages—and it is only for such a person that you are cataloging Thevet—can guess that this title page features ligatures and a sprinkling of different kinds and sizes of type. Such things are as common on early title pages as are noses and ears on post-office worthies.

But even an expert has no way of knowing the full content of the title page, the exact spelling of individual words, and the points at which the lines end.

These three things—content, spelling, and line endings—are normally enough to distinguish a title page. There are, for instance, two issues of John Dryden's *The Spanish Fryar or The Double Discovery* (London: Printed for R. Tonson and J. Tonson, 1681) whose title pages differ only in the subtitles: (1) "OR, THE/ DOUBLE/ DISCOVERY./"; (2) "OR,/ The Double Difcovery./." The difference in type is, of course, a distinguishing feature, but in a transcription the line endings alone would set them apart. Again, one 1640 edition of Francis Bacon's *Certaine Considerations* employs both roman and italic type, while the other, although worded exactly the same, has only roman. But there are also differences in ornaments (i.e., content), line endings, and spelling. There are two editions of the Church of England *Homilies* (London: Printed by R. H. and I. N. for R. Whitaker, 1640), one actually printed in 1640 but the other at least ten years later, apparently printed surreptitiously during the Commonwealth. Their title pages are phrased alike, but, in addition to typographical differences, their line endings differ, and in the imprint the later edition has an "S." where the other had "St." Similarly, there are two editions of *The Sentimental Song Book* (Grand Rapids, Mich.: C. M. Loomis, 1876) by Julia A. Moore, "the sweet singer of Michigan," one of them actually printed in 1893. The later title page differs somewhat in typography but also in that it has no period after "book"; the covers are reproduced and the title pages transcribed by A. H. Greenly in B.S.A. *Papers* 39: 91–118 (1945). Preferred copies of *Vanity Fair* (London, 1847–48) have the fifth line of the title page reading "With illustrations on steel and wood by the author," while in others the order is reversed, "wood and steel." None of these cases would require quasi-facsimile transcription.

If more than contents, spelling, and line endings is needed to set off a title page, the type seldom shows it. Quasi-facsimile transcriptions of the title pages of the two

1597 editions of Hugh Broughton's *Epistle to the Learned Nobilitie* (Middelburgh: R. Schilders, 1597), for instance, would be identical, yet the titles themselves are in different settings of type. This is true also of several of the Church of England *Homilies* dated 1547 and of a number of other books, both early and modern. Title-page transcriptions of the first three editions of the Lincoln-Douglas debates (1860) would be the same; cf. E. J. Wesson in B.S.A. *Papers* 40: 103–104 (1946). On the other hand, one may come across books like *An Apology for the Conduct of Mr. Charles Macklin* (London: Sold by T. Axtell, 1773) of which there are two issues with identical title pages but some differences in the content of the book itself. In his bibliography of Whittier (1937) and in that of Holmes (1953), Currier found it unnecessary to indicate title-page typography in order to distinguish editions and issues.

The fact is that, although transcription of the title page is quite important, the entire burden of separating issues and editions cannot be placed upon transcription alone. Adequate distinction will result only if the description of the rest of the book is also reasonably accurate.

Full Content Only

A library's collection of rare books may well be too small to justify changing a typewriter and having a typist master the different keyboard just to copy title pages. However, a transcription giving only full contents, exact spelling, and line endings will generally be as useful as quasi-facsimile. Such a transcription of the Thevet would run as follows:

> ¶ The new/ found vvorlde, or/ Antarctike, wherin is contai-/ ned wōderful and strange/ things, as well of humaine crea-/ tures, as beastes, fishes, foules, and ser-/ pents, trees, plants, mines of/ golde and siluer: garnished with/ many learned aucthorities,/ trauailed and written in the French/ tong, by that excellent learned/ man, master Andrevve/ Theuet./ And now newly translated into Englishe,/ wherein is reformed the errours of/ the auncient cosmo-/ graphers./ ¶ Imprinted

at London,/ by Henrie Bynneman, for/ Thomas Hacket./ And are to be sold at his shop in Poules church-/ yard, at the signe of the key./

Type

The entire text of the title page, it will be noted, is reduced to roman lower-case letters, using initial capitals only when absolutely necessary, that is, with proper nouns and adjectives and with the first word after a period. Adequate information about the kinds of type used may appear in a note—e.g., "Title in roman, italic, and black letter." The first word of a cited title or of an alternative title, such as that of Dryden's *Spanish Fryar* noted previously, would also have an initial capital. Punctuation is kept without change; some copies of Thomas L. Peacock's *Nightmare Abbey* (London: T. Hookham, Jr., 1818), for instance, have a colon after "abbey," while others do not.

Spelling

Spelling is reproduced exactly as it is on the title page. Thus, the two v's used for a w in "vvorlde" and in "ANDREVVE" are retained. Occasionally one may find that the printer has filed down the inner edges of the two letters until they look almost like the "W" in "NEW." In such a case, because the two letters were intended to serve always as one, they may be represented as simply "w"; but if there is any doubt, it is usually better to type "vv."

In most books printed prior to 1600 (and the practice changed then only gradually), V was the normal capital of both *v* and *u*, while in lower case *v* was used initially and *u* medially. "I" was used for what we now distinguish as I and J; there was, indeed, a lower-case J, but it seems to have been used only in the combination "*ij*." So in the transcription above "trauailed" is retained, while "THEVET" is reduced to "Theuet" according to what would have been contemporary usage. "VIVACIOUS,"

"IAMES," and "IVRY" would have been rendered "viuacious," "Iames," and "iury." "LAVVES," however, would be transcribed "lavves," not "lauues." If what the printer would have done is uncertain, the practice found to prevail elsewhere in the book may be followed.

Contracted forms such as "wōderful" should be retained; otherwise the reader would not know if they were in the book or not. McKerrow (319–24) has a useful discussion of the more common contractions and abbreviations. Frequently they can be represented with typewriter characters, but it is not at all difficult to draw them in when necessary.

Most spelling which would seem strange today—"vvorlde," "foules," "humaine," and so on—requires no comment by the cataloger. The early English printer allowed himself considerable freedom in spelling in order to make his lines of type exactly fill out the proper space. (This is called "justifying," and today it is done by the use of different-sized spaces between words in the line.) Thus in the Thevet title page we find "wherin," line 3, but "wherein," line 15.

Occasionally, however, genuine errors will be found, such as the following: (1) Duplication of letters—"boooke" in Peter Bales' *Writing Schoolemaster* (London: T. Orwin, 1590) and "writtten" in Matteo Bandello's *Certaine Tragicall Discourses* (London: T. Marshe, 1567); forms such as "heere" or "tvvoo" in Francis Bacon's *The Tvvoo Bookes* (London: Printed for H. Tomes, 1605) are of course permissible. (2) Omission of letters—"Chrisian" in Robert Abbot's *Holinesse of Chrisian Churches* (London: Printed by T. Paine for P. Stephens and C. Meredith, 1638) or "falsy" in Alexander Baillie's *True Information* (Wirtsburgh: A. M. Volmare, 1628). (3) Use of the wrong letter—"cectaine" in *Guide unto Sion* (Amsterdam, 1640) and (rather amusing to a modern reader) "the tight reuerend father" in Hugh Latimer's *Frutefull Sermons* (London: J. Day, 1575).

If it is certain that a queerly spelled word belongs to one of these three types of error, it may be followed by a bracketed "sic" or exclamation point; but if there is any doubt at all, it is best left alone. Cowley (66) prefers to leave errors entirely unmarked and to "expect the reader to believe that they are correctly transcribed." But he goes on to say that he himself places a checkmark in pencil above misprints copied into his notes "so as not to be assailed by doubts of my accuracy"!

Sometimes errors tell something of the history of the printing of a title page. In some copies of *A Helpe to Discourse* (13th ed.; London: Printed by B. A. and T. F. for N. Vavasour, 1640) the title reads "readded," line 11, and "aoe," line 3, of the imprint, while in other copies it is "re-added" and "are." Apparently both words were corrected during printing. Similarly in the title of Latimer's *27 Sermons* (London: J. Day, 1562), "apyoynted," line 10, was later corrected to "appoynted."

In sixteenth- and seventeenth-century titles one or two words may be in Greek or Hebrew characters. Such words can be drawn in, but the card will probably tend to be more accurate and will be neater looking if they are omitted or transliterated. If the latter, a note should so state.

Line Endings

The ending of each line is indicated by a single sloping stroke. In some early books the printers themselves used sloping strokes as marks of punctuation. In transcribing such a book's title it may be well to omit line endings and call attention to them in a note—e.g., "Lines end with book, block, and boy: the sloping strokes actually appear on the title page." It is possible, of course, to have a vertical stroke key added to the typewriter and use that for line endings; certainly this should be done if the typewriter is altered for quasi-facsimile transcriptions.

Line endings are sometimes hard to indicate. It was, for instance, rather common in seventeenth century books to tabulate items in a column on a title page and then join them by a brace. Probably the simplest solution is to reproduce the arrangement of this part of such a title page rather closely. Thus the title page of *A Banquet of Jests* (1657) would be transcribed:

> A/ banquet/ of jests/ new and old./ Or/ change of cheare./ Being/ a collection/
>
> of { modern jests
witty jeeres
pleasant taunts
merrie tales
>
> [rule]/ The last edition, much enlarged./ [rule]/ London,/ printed for R. Royston, at the angell/ in Ivy lane. 1657./

Sometimes a series of lengthy phrases or sentences, rather than a list of words, is similarly joined by a brace, as in Francis Bacon's *Three Speeches* (London: Printed by R. Badger for S. Broun, 1641), which the title page tells us were written:

> Concerning the { Post-nati
Naturalization of the Scotch in England
Vnion of the lawes of the kingdomes of England and Scotland.

An alternative to close reproduction would be to transcribe the bracketed portion of *A Banquet of Jests* thus:

> collection/ of/ modern jests/ witty jeeres/ pleasant taunts/ merrie tales./

This, however, would indicate an arrangement of the text different from that actually employed by the printer unless it were accompanied by a cumbersome note of explanation—e.g., "The phrases 'modern jests, witty jeeres, pleasant taunts, merrie tales' are in a column joined by a brace opposite the word 'of'." Another possibility is the system used in the Union Theological Seminary's *Catalogue of the McAlpin Collection* (New York, 1927–30) by which the pertinent section of Bacon's *Three Speeches* would be transcribed thus:

> Concerning the {Post-nati/ Naturalization of the Scotch in/ England/ Vnion of the lawes of the kingdomes/ of England and Scotland./

Neither alternative is as clear as close reproduction, and probably neither saves much time or space.

Occasionally a title occupies more than one page. The title of the first edition of George Ade's *Fables in Slang* might be transcribed as follows:

> Fables/ [rule]/ in/ [rule]/ slang/[rule]/ by/ George/ Ade/ [title completed on opposite page] illustrated/ by/ Clyde J./ Newman/ [rule]/ published by/ Herbert S. Stone/ and company/ Chicago & New York/ MDCCCC/
>
> (The title page is reproduced in D. R. Russo's *George Ade* opposite p.32.)

Sometimes the title is in two or more columns, each in a different language. The title pages of some of Sir Edward Coke's *Reports* have English and Latin versions in parallel columns. In such a case it is usually sufficient to transcribe fully only the English title and add in a note: "Latin title in a column parallel with the English."

Omissions

The New Found Worlde has a title which is long, but not too long to be transcribed entirely. For rare books the cataloger's primary concern, of course, is that the title transcription show how a particular book differs from all other books, and it occasionally happens that a point of distinction occurs precisely in a nonessential item. For instance, there are three issues of Thomas Otway's *Friendship in Fashion* (London: Printed by E. F. for R. Tonson, 1678) whose title-page transcriptions differ in line 11: (1) "Licenced, May 31. Roger Le 'Estrange [no period]"; (2) "Licenced May 31. 1678. Roger L 'Estrange."; (3) "Licenced, &c." Even mottoes can be of importance. There are two issues of Henry Crosse's *Vertues Commonwealth* (London: Printed for J. Newbery, 1603) whose title pages are partially in different settings of type and have some line endings and some words different. The last two features would be enough to set the issues apart, but the Latin motto, which is in the same setting of type in both issues, appears in one with a word incorrectly spelled. Probably the state of the title page with the correct spelling is the later.

The title page of Francis Bacon's *Essaies* (London: Printed for J. Jaggard, 1613) gives the author's name and also describes him as a knight and the king's attorney general. For so famous an author it might seem reasonable to omit his titles, as, indeed, was done by W. C. Hazlitt in his *Bibliographical Collections,* 3d series, 2d supplement (London: B. Quaritch, 1892), 6. But there are three editions of this year, and their title-page transcriptions differ only in the spelling of "attorney." Because their collations are identical, it is now impossible to know which edition Hazlitt described.

Omitted portions of the title should be indicated. Three dots may show the omission of less than a line, but if one line or more is omitted, it will be helpful to make clear just how much is lacking. Thus, if the *New Found Worlde* title were three or four times as long as it actually is and some abbreviation seemed necessary, we might have:

> The new/ found vvorlde, or/ Antarctike. . ./ [6 lines] . . . written in the French/ tong, by . . ./ . . . Andrewe/ etc.

Insertions

All information or comment which the transcriber inserts in the title is best set off by brackets—e.g., [6 lines] or [!]. If some of the title is actually printed within brackets, a note to that effect is necessary. Thus, for J. V. Long's *Report of the First General Festival of the Renowned Mormon Battalion* (Salt Lake City: Printed at the Deseret News Office, 1855), one might write a note somewhat as follows: "The tenth line of the title, '[reported by J. V. Long.],' is actually printed within brackets."

It is, of course, conventional for catalogers to indicate such brackets thus ⟨ ⟩, but it is highly doubtful if anyone except another cataloger will understand what is meant by this device. Greg (*Bibl.* vol.4, p.cxxxi) uses "brackets . . . of a heavier sort" to indicate brackets actually on the title page; this is possible only in a printed bibliography or a printed catalog, and like the cataloger's conventional device, it might be understood only by another cataloger.

Ornaments and Devices

Ornamentation is rather frequent on early title pages. Small figures, such as the two paragraph marks of *The New Found Worlde,* can be drawn in with little trouble. The same is true of hands, flowers, leaves, and so on. Other features, such as horizontal rules, rows of tiny type ornaments or one or more larger ornaments between sections of the title page, may be described with the simple statement "rule" or "2 rules" or "row of type ornaments" inserted, within brackets, at the proper place in the transcription. Another portion of Bacon's *Three Speeches* would be transcribed: "Scotland./ [rule]/ Published by the authors copy,/ and/ licensed by authority./ [rule]/ London,/" etc.

In printed bibliographies a note of ornamentation is sometimes abbreviated—e.g., "///" instead of "/[rule]/" or "[orn.]" instead of "[ornament]." Such abbreviations can be explained once and for all in an introduction to a printed bibliography, but on a catalog card it is best to write out in full an easily understood statement because an abbreviation would be clear only to someone familiar with the cataloger's system.

Sometimes an ornament can be identified as a printer's or publisher's device and it should be so described—"[printer's device]."

There may be a row of type ornaments or a single ornament (but seldom if ever a printer's device) at the top of the title page, as in Lancelot Andrewes' *Copie of the Sermon* (London: R. Barker, 1604) or John Harrison's *Late Newes out of Barbary* (London: Imprinted for A. Jonson, 1613). The first word or first few words of the title may be on an ornamental block, as in Thomas Middleton's *Phoenix* (London: Printed by E. A. for A. I., 1607), which also has an ornament at the head of its title; or they may be within a decorative frame, as in *Arthur of Brytayn* (London: R. Redborne, [1555?]) and Johann Habermann's *Enimie of Securitie* ([London]: 1579). The first letter of the title of John Coke's *Debate betwene the Heraldes* ([London]: R. Wyer, 1550) is an ornamental initial occupying two lines; this practice, however, is unusual. All ornamentation at the opening of the title may be presented within brackets at the close of the transcription or, if the description is lengthy or involved, in a note. In printed bibliographies such information is normally presented before the transcription, but this location on a catalog card would result in filing difficulties.

Title-Page Borders

The title-page border enjoyed great popularity in early books. It could be quite simple, like the border of type ornaments used for the *New Found Worlde;* or it might be composed merely of one or more rules like that used with Nostradamus' almanac (fig. 8) or with George Ade's *Peggy from Paris* (1903). But often it was an elaborate frame cut on wood or metal employing geometrical or floral designs, often combined with mythological figures, or a series of pictures, as in the border used with early editions of John Foxe's famous book of martyrs.

The martyrs border illustrates the text, but often enough the early printer made no attempt to fit a border to the subject of the book. One border, for instance, has a stag's head flanked by two naked boys at the top, Diana and Minerva standing at either side, and, at the foot, between two rabbits, a panel showing Diana bathing and Actaeon being transformed into a stag while the angry goddess casts water upon him. (It is reproduced in R. B. McKerrow and F. S. Ferguson's *Title-Page Borders Used in England & Scotland 1485–1640* (London: Printed for the Bibliographical Soc. at the Oxford Univ. Pr., 1932, no. 215.) This was used, appropriately enough perhaps, with *Willobie His Auisa* (London: J. Windet, 1594) and later with several other purely literary works. But it was also used with such solemn tomes as Jean Taffin's *Amendment of Life* (London: G. Bishop, 1595), Richard Turnbull's *Exposition upon . . . Saint Iames* (London: Printed by J. Windet, sold by R. Bankworth, 1606), Francis Quarles' *Sions Elegies* (London: Printed by W. Stansby for T. Dewe, 1625), and even with the Sternhold and Hopkins *Psalmes* (London: Printed for the Company of Stationers, 1641).

Engraved Title Pages

If the printer wanted something more elaborate, he could have his title page entirely engraved. The engraved title page tends to be more involved. The title page to Abraham Darcie's translation of William Camden's *Annals* (London: Printed for B. Fisher, 1625), for instance (fig. 2), is flanked on each side by three pillars each bearing five noblemen's coats of arms; in each corner is represented a victorious battle with the Spaniards; at the top are a crowned Tudor rose and a phoenix, both emblematic of Queen Elizabeth; while at the bottom are another row of noblemen's shields and a distorted map of Spain and South America. Sometimes the engraved title page appears in addition to a printed title page whose text may be quite different, as with Thomas Coryate's *Crudities* (London: W. S., 1611) engraved by William Hole, which features the author's portrait and humorous representations of various adventures which had befallen him on his travels.

In more modern times the engraved title page has fallen into disuse, but hand-lettered titles are even today by no means uncommon. George Ade's *Fables in Slang* (1900), noted above, is on a two-page spread, hand-lettered, the whole within a decorative border.

How to Describe Ornamentation

With the exception of simple rules or type ornaments, title-page ornamentation can generally be described adequately only in the notes. It is helpful, however, if, at the proper place in the transcription, a bracketed allusion to the ornamentation refers the reader to this descriptive note—e.g., "Printer's mark; see below," or "The whole within a border; see below," or "Title page engraved; see below." Sometimes one can locate a reproduction or an elaborate description; if so, he can simply refer to it. If a reproduction cannot be found, it will be helpful to give a brief description and measurement in millimeters, giving vertical measurement first.

Adequate description of an ornament or printer's device

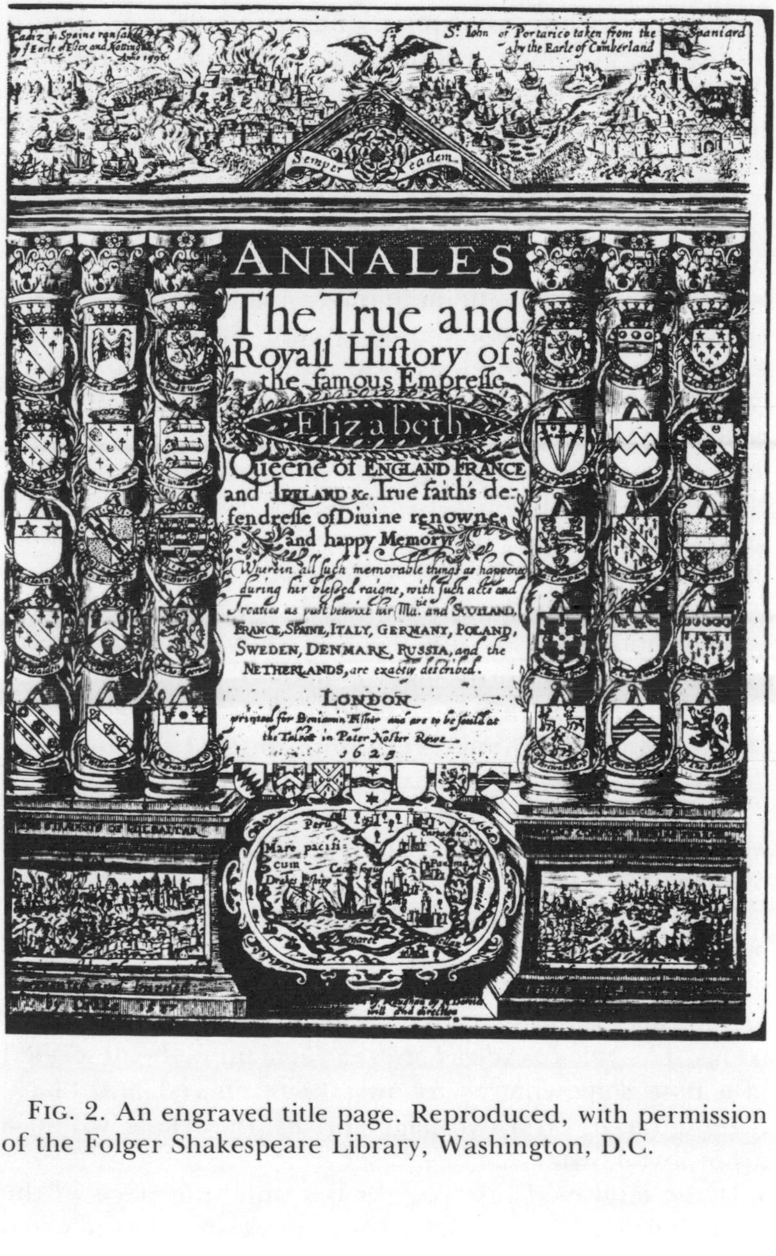

FIG. 2. An engraved title page. Reproduced, with permission of the Folger Shakespeare Library, Washington, D.C.

may consist of the inscription and/or initials used with it or, if there are none, a short statement of its outstanding features. Thus the printer's mark of John Day, which is reproduced as no. 128 in R. B. McKerrow's *Printers' & Publishers' Devices* (London: Printed for the Bibliographical Soc. at the Chiswick Pr., 1913), could be described as follows: "Printer's mark 107 × 78 mm.: 'Vivet tamen post funera virtus' and 'Etsi mors, indies accelerat.' " If there were no inscription, the note might read: "Printer's mark 107 × 78 mm. skeleton, tree, two men." Such a description will generally be enough to show if the ornament or device is the same as that in another copy of the book. If there is no inscription and if the ornament cannot be described in three or four words, it is best to give only the size. Never give an allegorical or mythological interpretation unless you are quite certain that it is correct; otherwise the note may cause no little confusion.

The same principles apply to the description of title-page borders and engraved title pages, except that a maximum of ten or twelve words may be allowed if the subject is complicated. The title-page border showing Actaeon and Diana (McKerrow and Ferguson, no. 215) might be described: "Title within border 167 × 113 mm.: At bottom a panel showing woman bathing, man with stag's head watching." The following note would serve for the title page of Camden's *Annals:* "Title page engraved by R. Vaughan 216 × 160 mm.: Pillars at sides, battles in corners, map at bottom."

Not infrequently some words in early titles are printed in red, and some two-color titles occur even in modern books. The title of Ade's *Fables in Slang* might be described in a note somewhat as follows: "Title in red and black, hand-lettered, on a two-page spread, the whole within a decorative border."

If the engraved title page is the only title page in the book, it will, of course, have been transcribed in the usual place, but if it appears in addition to the printed title page, its transcription is best relegated to the note describing it. In such a case it is generally enough to transcribe only that part of the engraved title page which may give information not on the main title page. The title page of Coryate's *Crudities,* noted above, might be entirely transcribed. However, the only major difference between the two title pages of Richard Brathwait's *Two Lancashire Lovers* (1640) is their imprints: (1) Printed title page: "London,/ printed by Edward Griffin./ For R. B. or his assignes./ 1640./"; (2) Engraved title page: "London,/ printed/ by E. G./ for R. Best/ and are to be sould/ at his shop neare/ Graies Inn gate in/ Houlbourne./."

Imprints

The imprint of a rare book may be considerably more important than that of an ordinary book and is transcribed exactly as it stands with no attempt to reduce it to the formula: place, publisher, date. Two issues of John Dryden's *Troilus and Cressida,* printed at London in 1679 for Abel Swall and Jacob Tonson, have title pages differing only in that one imprint names Swall first while the other names Tonson first. Roman numerals should be retained in the transcription.

In the late seventeenth century and during the eighteenth century an imprint often named many publishers, and the cataloger has a strong temptation to omit some of them, or at least their addresses. It is sometimes safer to retain their entire content, however, because the only difference between one issue and another—or at least the difference most easily shown—is in the imprint. There are two issues of Shakespeare's *Hamlet* (1695) differing in their imprints: (1) "London:/ printed for H. Herringman, and R. Bentley; and sold/ by R. Bentley, J. Tonson, T. Bennet, and F. Sanders./ MDCXCV./"; (2) "London:/ printed for R. Bentley in Russel-street in Covent-garden./ MDCXCV./." The title pages of two issues of *Shakespeare's History of the Times* (London: Printed for D. Browne and J. Murray, 1778) differ only in that one gives Browne's address and the other does not. The transcriptions of two issues of John Dryden's *Conquest of Granada* (6th ed., 1704) would be identical if only the first name, or even the first two names, of each imprint were included: (1) "London,/ printed for J. Tonson and T. Bennet: and sold by R. Wel-/ lington, G. Strahan, and B. Lintott. 1704./"; (2) "London,/ printed for J. Tonson, and T. Bennet: and sold by J. Knap-/ ton at the Crown in St. Paul's church-yard, G. Strahan and/ W. Davis over-against the Royal exchange in Cornhill. 1704./."

Apart from the fact that printers' and publishers' names and addresses in an imprint may distinguish a book from other issues and editions, it is often helpful to the student of printing history to learn that some man or group of men was doing business in a particular place at a specific date. Such information is especially useful in the study of undated books which give the names and addresses of printers and publishers.

Colophons

The imprint of the *New Found Worlde* records the place, printer, bookseller, and his address; it omits the printer's address and the date. For these we turn to the end of the book to what is called the "colophon": "¶ Imprinted at London, in Knight-/ rider strete, by Henry Bynneman, for/ Thomas Hacket./ 1568./."

On the catalog card the colophon is in a paragraph immediately following the transcription of the title page, introduced thus: "Colophon, T4 recto: ¶ Imprinted [etc.]." All transcriptions of the colophon or any other part of the text of the book should be in the same style as that used for the title-page transcription; otherwise, some confusion may result. Ornamentation, omissions, and inserted material are to be noted just as with the title. It is necessary to tell the location (T4 recto—the meaning of this symbol will be discussed in the next chapter) because often the colophon does not come at the very end of the book. Sometimes the colophon merely repeats the information given in the imprint. If this were the case with the *New Found Worlde* and if the statement were unduly long, it would probably be sufficient merely to write: "Colophon, T4 recto."

In early books the colophon normally recorded the printer's and/or publisher's name and address and the date. Gradually this information was transferred to the title-page imprint, and during the seventeenth century the colophon fell into disuse. In nineteenth and twentieth century books the title-page imprint often tells only the publisher, and on the verso of the title page or at the end of the book there may be a statement (sometimes quite elaborate) of precisely by whom, from what materials, where, and when the book was produced. There is a tendency to call this statement a "printer's imprint" and to transcribe it only in the analysis of the book's content on the ground that "since the printer has ceased to be concerned directly in the publication of books, his identity is rarely of bibliographical significance" (Cowley, 84).

On the other hand, it is by no means certain that all early printers differed from their modern brethren in that they were always "concerned directly in the publication of books," and many early booksellers seem to have done little if any actual printing. Again, the rare book is valuable chiefly, if not entirely, as a physical entity. Surely the making of that physical entity is as important as having it made or selling it after it has been made. So it seems more logical always to locate and transcribe any statement concerning the making or publishing of the book, if it does not appear on the title page, in a paragraph immediately following the imprint for modern books no less than for early books. It might be desirable, however, to call such a statement a "colophon" only when it comes near the end of the book and a "printer's imprint" when it occurs somewhere else, such as the verso of the title page. The "imprimatur" notice of an earlier book (if it is not on the title page, of course) and the copyright notice of a modern book might be given in this paragraph also.

Occasionally one will come across a book without a title page. Many incunabula as well as pamphlets and folders and even books in modern times have been so printed.

For such a book a statement of title, printer, and date will take the place of the usual transcribed title and imprint; or the caption title or running title (if there is one) may be transcribed fully. For an incunabulum such a statement may include a transcription of the first few lines of actual text, the first line of the second gathering of actual text, and the last few lines of actual text. The colophon, of course, will be transcribed in full, because it may well contain some information which would normally be found on the title page.

If the book is simply defective with the title page missing, the cataloger may be able to find a transcription in some bibliography, or his library may even wish to purchase a photostat or microfilm of the missing leaf. He should acknowledge the source of his transcription in a note. If he cannot locate a transcription or get microfilms or photostats of another copy, the caption title or running title will have to do.

Calculated Risk

Quasi-facsimile and even full content only are both rather expensive because each requires a highly trained, scholarly cataloger to spend much time in the mechanical drudgery of transcribing and then proofreading titles which may be quite long. Are these methods worth the trouble and expense? The conventional defense of elaborate transcription of either kind is that such transcription is needed to distinguish a book in hand from other editions and issues of the same work, some (or many) of which may be unknown to the cataloger or even the bibliographer. There seems to be some evidence that this may not generally be the case.

In 1946 the LC *Studies* attacked the logic of full and elaborate transcription for ordinary books. The pamphlet included (p.36–39) a report by Elizabeth Pierce of an experiment with 2,504 main entries representing 198 titles: "No entry failed to be identified through the simplified cataloging when it would have been identified through full transcription." Full transcription, whether quasi-facsimile or full content only, is thus not necessary to identify editions and issues. Indeed, "the element indicating reliably an edition or issue is not on the title-page but in the collation: the main paging."

Foxon shows that quasi-facsimile transcription seems to have been devised independently by two men: Edward Capell in the eighteenth century and Falconer Madan in the late nineteenth century, each of them wanting solely to "help the reader visualize the title—an antiquarian interest for Capell, a desire to show changes in layout in historical perspective for Madan" (p.18). The idea that elaborate transcription is a means of distinguishing editions and issues Foxon considers only a rationalization of an already existing practice. With a study of Greg's bibliography he found that "in almost every case a straightforward transcription of the title in roman type (without line endings) and the collation suffices to distinguish editions; only in three cases out of about a thousand is quasi-facsimile transcription necessary to distinguish editions, and in three further cases it fails to do the job" (p.19). This seems to justify what we have called full content only. Foxon quotes with approval Falconer Madan's suggestion that "the readiest method of distinguishing a reprint from a reissue is to note the exact position of the signatures on a few pages in relation to the letters of the text immediately above them. A re-printer never adheres precisely to the usage of the original edition" (p.18). (By "reprint" Madan apparently meant what we have above defined as "edition." We shall discuss collation, signatures and gatherings in later chapters.)

Francis F. Madan's bibliography of the *Eikon Basilike* describes eighty-one editions of the work dated 1648–1904; a number of these editions consist of two or more issues each. Of these editions and issues only twenty have each the same collation and pagination as that of the entry immediately preceding—i.e., probably almost all but twenty can be individually identified by collation and pagination without regard to title transcription. Of these twenty entries for editions and issues, seven would differ from their preceding entries if they had a brief title transcription, four would require quasi-facsimile, and nine would require descriptive notes regardless of how the title were transcribed—e.g., "no.1, third issue" differs from "no.1, second issue" in that the pagination of gathering G is corrected.

Madan has entries for thirty-nine editions dated 1648 or 1649. Of these thirty-nine editions eight have two issues each, six have three issues each, and twenty-five have no variant issues; thus, thirty-nine editions exist in a total of fifty-nine versions. Madan's "Key for Identification of Editions" is in terms of the paging of the *Eikon* section alone in the thirty-nine editions. There are twenty-five different paginations for the *Eikon* section, and only eight of these paginations are common to more than one edition; twenty-four editions existing in thirty versions are involved in these eight paginations. Of these thirty versions not identified by the *Eikon* section paging alone, seventeen would be identified by adding only the collation and paging of the entire book, one would be identified by quasi-facsimile transcription, eight would be identified by full-content-only transcription, and four would require descriptive notes no matter how the title was transcribed—e.g., "no.12, first issue" differs from no.11 only in that the title page is respaced and gatherings A–D, F, H, and the inner form of gathering G are reset.

The LC *Studies,* the Foxon study, and an examination of the Madan bibliography seem to indicate that:

1. Although quasi-facsimile transcription or full-content-only transcription would, indeed, help identify editions and issues more fully, the number of editions and issues of any work requiring full transcription of either kind is quite small.

2. Collation by gatherings and pagination are much more important than title transcription in identifying editions and issues.

3. There are some editions and issues which cannot be identified even by quasi-facsimile or full-content-only transcription and collation by gatherings and pagination;

in addition, they require descriptive notes to identify them.

These three suggestions lead to a fourth: the cataloger will save a lot of time and money if he takes a calculated risk with title transcription. Probably transcription can be simpler and briefer than full content only. It is true that on occasion he will fail to identify an edition or issue; that is the risk. But it will not happen often. Moreover, it is not unlikely that the scholar wanting to use the book would insist on making his own judgment about its edition and issue anyhow. All he would ask of the cataloger would be to have the book in the catalog under an entry he could find and to have it described enough to arouse his curiosity.

Calculated-risk transcription seems to mean something along the following lines:

1. Follow regular cataloging practice with regard to capitals and punctuation; that is, treat the title as if it were a sentence. Follow the spelling as indicated on pages 22–24. Do not indicate line endings.

2. Do not repeat the author's name unless there is more than one author. If there are more than three authors, include only the first three and indicate the other(s) by "[et al.]"

3. Transcribe only as much of the title as is necessary to show in broad terms what the book is about. If the title tends to be a table of contents, much of the detail may be omitted. Indicate each omission by three dots.

4. Enclose information not on the title page within brackets.

5. Include statement of edition or impression—e.g., "3d ed." or "2d impr."

6. List only the first place of publication, only the first printer, only the first publisher. Indicate others by "[etc.]"

7. Use only arabic numerals for the date.

Transcription of *The New Found Worlde* title by such a system would be as follows:

> The new found vvorlde, or Antarctike, wherin is contained wōderful and strange things . . . written in the French . . . and now newly translated into Englishe . . . London, Henrie Bynneman for Thomas Hacket [1568]

Such a transcription, of course, would leave unanswered most questions like those about specific books listed above (p.20–34); on the other hand, it is probable that *The New Found Worlde* may not raise them. This is the calculated risk.

Photographic Reproduction

Madan's bibliography of the *Eikon Basilike* uses photographic reproduction of titles, and this is often the case in printed bibliographies. Photographic reproduction saves a great deal of time; it is accurate; it more exactly shows the kinds and relative sizes of type and ornaments; and there is no need to agonize over what to omit from a transcription. With photographic reproduction of the title and collation by gatherings and pagination the cataloger has done all he can short of handing the reader the book itself.

Bowers admitted the advantages of photographic reproduction, but he felt that it would never completely replace quasi-facsimile transcription because photographic reproductions are themselves susceptible to error—e.g., imperfect copies chosen for reproduction, imperfections in the paper, incorrect retouching (because of incorrect interpreting) of smudged portions, etc. (p.135–37). The same kind of errors, of course, can also be copied into quasi-facsimile transcriptions, and in addition, typographical errors may be overlooked in proofreading.

Photographic reproduction can, of course, be used in printed catalogs as well as in printed bibliographies. It can even be used on catalog cards, although the reproduction may be somewhat awkwardly placed and with small type sometimes difficult to read (see Philip J. Weimerskirch, "The Use of Title-Page Photography in Cataloging," *Library Resources and Technical Services* 12: 37–46 [1968]).

So much for transcription. Quasi-facsimile or full content only are traditional, and they offer many advantages, but they are costly. Calculated-risk transcription is much cheaper and does almost as complete a job. Photographic reproduction seems best of all.

5. While Thumbing through the Leaves: Format

Often a man does not have a wart on his nose or an Andy Gump chin; in fact, his face may at times seem rather like the face of some other man, particularly some other man in his family. So we have found it is with a book: its title page alone is seldom enough to set it apart from other books, particularly from other editions, issues, or printings of the same work.

The post-office poster does more than display a face; it proclaims that the face belongs to a body which is tall or short, fat or lean, lacks a finger or sprouts an extra toe. Books have bodies, too.

Format

The size, shape, and general appearance of a book we call its "format." The basic unit of a book is a gathering of leaves produced by folding a part of a large sheet of paper, a whole sheet, or several sheets. In an early book each gathering was sewed at its middle fold to cords across the spine of the book and these cords were attached to the covers. If the book was rather thin, it might have been "stabbed" (i.e., sewed through sideways, much as is done with magazines) to hold the gatherings together. So the format of a book depends on: (1) the size of the original sheets, (2) the number of times each sheet was folded, (3) the number of sheets in a gathering, and (4) the number of gatherings in a book.

Paper

Until the close of the eighteenth century all paper was made by hand one sheet at a time. Linen and cotton rags were beaten to a pulp and stirred with water. Workmen then dipped out the mixture in shallow trays or "molds" with wire bottoms and removable wooden sides called "deckles." As each mold was lifted, the water drained away, but the pulp settled in a thin layer on the wire bottom and the mold was shaken in such a way that the fibers interlocked, forming a sheet of paper.

The size of the mold, of course, determined the size of the sheet. There seems to have been some variety in the size of the sheet even in early books. William Caxton, for instance, used sheets as large as 15¾ × 22 inches and as small as 11 × 16; when John Day printed the large folio volumes of Foxe's *Actes and Monuments* (London, 1570) he used two sizes of paper, one exactly twice as large as the other. Generally speaking, however, the sheet was at first rather small and then became steadily larger after the middle of the seventeenth century.

The edges of the sheet were rough and uneven where the pulp had come against the deckles; they may be seen in the sheet illustrated in figure 3. They were frequently cut away when the book was bound, but today many people think deckle edges attractive and they are sometimes artificially produced on machine-made paper.

Chain Lines and Watermarks

The wire bottom of the mold impressed a design on the sheet which can be seen if the paper is held up to the light. In the one-sheet "Proclamation" (fig. 3), for instance, there are eighteen rather regularly spaced heavy lines running across the sheet (A to B); these are called "chain lines." At right angles to these lines are other fainter lines very much closer together; in this particular sheet there are about twenty-eight of them to the inch. These lines which run the length of the sheet (C to D) are called "wire lines." Generally, but not always, there is also a "watermark," a device or symbol located at or near the middle of one half of the sheet. In modern paper, and in some old paper, it is the maker's trademark, but the

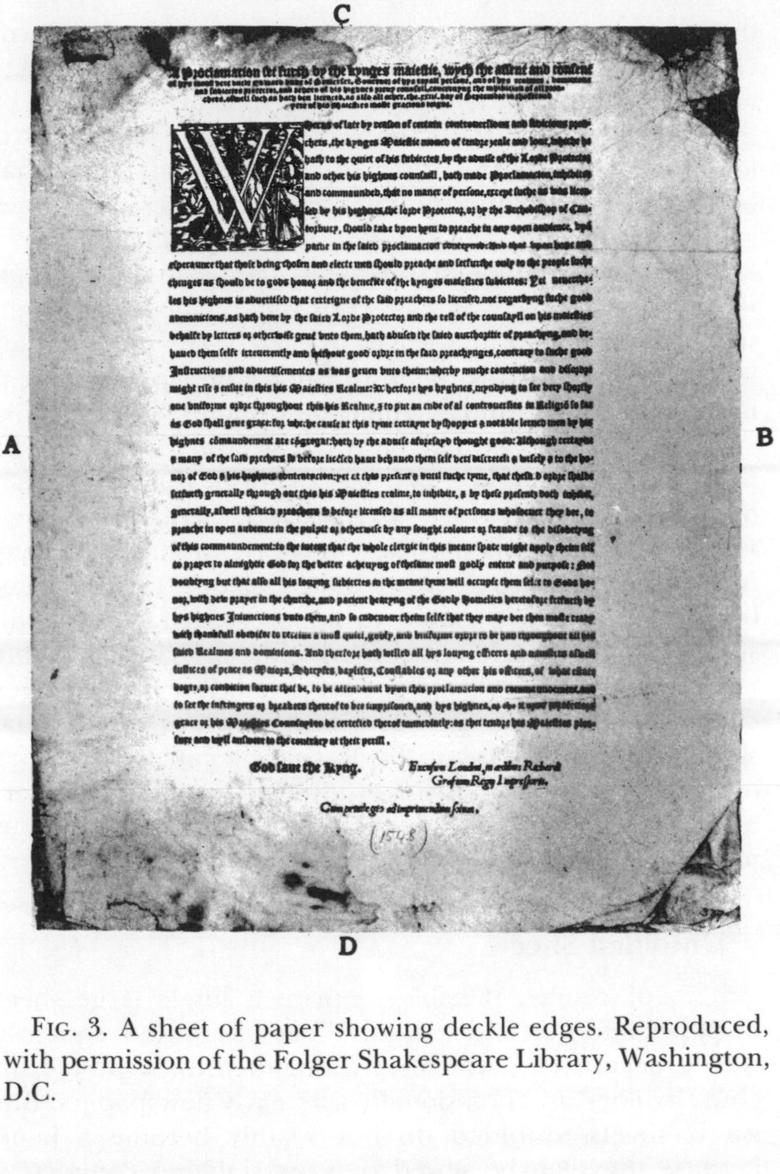

A Proclamation set furth by the kynges maiestie, wyth the assent and consent [illegible]

Whereas of late by reason of certain controuersious and seditious preachers, the kynges Maiestie moued of tendre zeale and loue, whiche he hath to the quiet of his subiectes, by the aduise of the Lorde Protector and other his highnes counsaill, hath made Proclamacion, inhibited and commaunded, that no maner of persone, except suche as was licensed by his highnes, the lorde Protector, or by the Archebishop of Cantorbury, should take upon hym to preache in any open audience, upon payne in the said proclamacion conteyned: And that upon hope and esperaunce that those being chosen and electe men should preache and setfurthe only to the people suche thinges as should be to gods honor and the benefite of the kynges maiesties subiectes: Yet neuertheles his highnes is aduertised that certeigne of the said preachers so licensed, not regardyng suche good admonicions, as hath bene by the saied Lorde Protector and the rest of the counsayll on his maiesties behalfe by letters or otherwise geuen unto them, hath abused the saied authoritie of preachyng, and behaued them selfe irreuerently and without good order in the said preachynges, contrary to suche good Instructions and aduertisementes as was geuen unto them: wherby muche contencion and disorder might rise and ensue in this his Maiesties Realme: Wherfore hys hyghnes, myndyng to see very shortly one uniforme order throughout this his Realme, and to put an ende of al controuersies in Religiō so farre as God shall geue grace: for whiche cause at this tyme certayne byshoppes and notable lerned men by his highnes cōmaundement are cōgregat: hath by the aduise aforesayd thought good: Although certayne and many of the said preachers so before licēced haue behaued them self veri discretel and wisely and to the honor of God and his highnes contentacion: yet at this present and until suche tyme, that the said order shalbe setfurth generally through out this his Maiesties realme, to inhibite, and by these presentz doth inhibit, generally, aswell the saied preachers so before licensed as all maner of persones whosoeuer they bee, to preache in open audience in the pulpit or otherwise by any sought colour or fraude to the disobeying of this commaundement: to the intent that the whole clergie in this meane space might apply theim self to prayer to almightie God for the better acheuyng of the same most godly entent and purpose: Not doubtyng but that also all his louyng subiectes in the meane tyme will occupie them selfe to Gods honor, with dew prayer in the churche, and pacient hearyng of the Godly Homelies heretofore setfurth by hys highnes Iniunctions unto them, and so endeuour theim selfe that they maye bee then moste ready with thankfull obedience to receiue a most quiet, godly, and uniforme order to be had throughout all his saied Realmes and dominions. And therfore hath willed all hys louyng officers and ministers aswell iustices of peace as Maiors, Sherypfes, bayliffes, Constables or any other his officers, of what estate degre, or condicion soeuer thei be, to be attendaunt upon this proclamacion and commaundement, and to see the infringers or breakers therof to bee imprisoned, and hys highnes, or the Lorde Protectors grace or his Maiesties Counsayle to be certefied therof immediatly: as thei tendre his Maiesties pleasure and will answere to the contrary at their perill.

God saue the Kyng.

Excusum Londini, in aedibus Richardi Graftoni Regii Impressoris.

Cum privilegio ad imprimendum solum.

(1548)

FIG. 3. A sheet of paper showing deckle edges. Reproduced, with permission of the Folger Shakespeare Library, Washington, D.C.

true significance of most early watermarks is unknown. Occasionally there is another device, the "countermark," located in the middle of the other half of the sheet. In the "Proclamation" sheet the watermark is a jug, and it is located a little to the right of, and extends somewhat below, the ornamental initial W. (Chain lines, wire lines and watermarks do not appear in the reproduction.)

If a cataloger understands what happens to the chain lines and watermark of a sheet of handmade paper when that sheet is folded into leaves in each of the possible patterns, he understands the most important single problem in the examination and adequate description of a rare book.

The original sheet may be twice as large as normal; or the gathering may be made up of more than one sheet or of less than one sheet; or the deckle edges and even most of the margins may be cut away; or the book may be sewed or glued so tightly that the cataloger cannot possibly see what leaf is joined to another. In fact, one will seldom find an early book in which some, and probably most, of these things have not occurred. But if a cataloger can follow the chain lines and watermark of the original sheet in and out among the leaves, he can tell whether or not any leaves are missing or inserted, and he can generally tell about what size that sheet was originally and how many times, and in what directions, it was folded.

Unfolded Sheets

It is, of course, possible to print a single large sheet of paper and not fold it at all. That was done frequently with proclamations which were intended to be posted on church doors, and occasionally with early newspapers. But single sheets unfolded do not readily become a book because they can be sewed only by stabbing completely through the left margin of the book and then stitching; this would bring undue strain at the inner margin of each sheet, and so tall a book so tightly bound would be quite inconvenient for the reader, particularly if it were at all thick. Stevenson, however, remarks (p.cliv) that precisely such a format was not uncommon among eighteenth- and nineteenth-century books with many color plates.

The smaller sheets in Foxe's *Actes and Monuments,* mentioned earlier, were each the size of a single leaf, and John Day had to use them after his supply of large sheets had run out. These single-sheet leaves could not very well have been stabbed and stitched because the rest of the book was sewed normally. Before printing, however, the small sheets had been pasted together at their edges in pairs so that each pair of sheets thus pasted could be handled as one single large sheet the size of those he had used in the rest of the book. But this practice was most unusual and may have been unique.

Talk of folding means very little unless one does the folding oneself. What follows will be much clearer if for each type of gathering the reader will take a sheet of typewriter-size paper (it would be more in proportion if it were somewhat shorter), draw in chain lines and watermark, and then fold it as indicated.

Folios

The simplest gathering is a folio in two leaves, illustrated (figs. 4 and 5) by the pamphlet *An Impartial Account* (London: Printed for Sam. Miller, 1680). Here a single sheet of paper has been printed in such a way that, when it is folded once parallel with the short side, along line AB, it forms a gathering of two leaves. The top side of a leaf is called its "recto"; the other side is the "verso." The recto of a leaf is a page, the verso is another page; each leaf, then, has two pages.

If leaf 1 recto had been text instead of a title page, the text would have begun on 1 recto, continued on 1 verso, then on 2 recto, and finally on 2 verso. At the bottom of 2 recto in a line by itself is printed the syllable "ing?"; this is called a "catchword," and it is the same as the first word or syllable of the next page of text, in this case 2 verso. The type which prints one side of a sheet is called a "form," and for this reason it is customary to refer to one side of a printed sheet also as a "form." The side which contains the first recto leaf in the sheet is called the "outer form," while the other side is called the "inner form." The outer form of this sheet (fig. 4) consists of 1 recto and 2 verso; the inner form (fig. 5) is composed of 1 verso and 2 recto.

The chain lines in this sheet run roughly parallel to the fold AB and the watermark is located in the middle of the second leaf. In a folio leaf, then, the chain lines are vertical, and in one of two conjugate folio leaves there is a watermark at the center unless, of course, the original sheet had no watermark. Occasionally there is a slight slant to the chain lines. Such a slant in one folio leaf should be matched by a slant in the leaf with which it is conjugate. Also the distance between chain lines in one folio leaf should be roughly (but only roughly) the same as the distance between chain lines in the leaf with which it is conjugate.

A gathering of only two folio leaves is rather unusual except in the late seventeenth and the eighteenth centuries. Because every gathering is sewed through its middle fold, a large book made up of two-leaf gatherings would require more of the binder's time for sewing, and the extra thread would cause the volume to bulge at the spine. Folio gatherings of four, six, or even eight leaves are more common. A folio gathering of four leaves was produced by folding two sheets together, six leaves by folding three sheets, and eight leaves by folding four sheets. In a four-leaf folio gathering leaves 1 and 2 are conjugate with 4 and 3; in a six-leaf gathering 1, 2, and 3 are conjugate with 6, 5, and 4; and in an eight-leaf gathering 1, 2, 3, and 4 are conjugate with 8, 7, 6, and 5.

Quartos

The quarto (4to) gathering of four leaves (figs. 6 and 7) appears in Archbishop William Laud's *Speech* (London: R. Badger, 1637). The original sheet is printed in such a way that it can be folded along line AB and then along

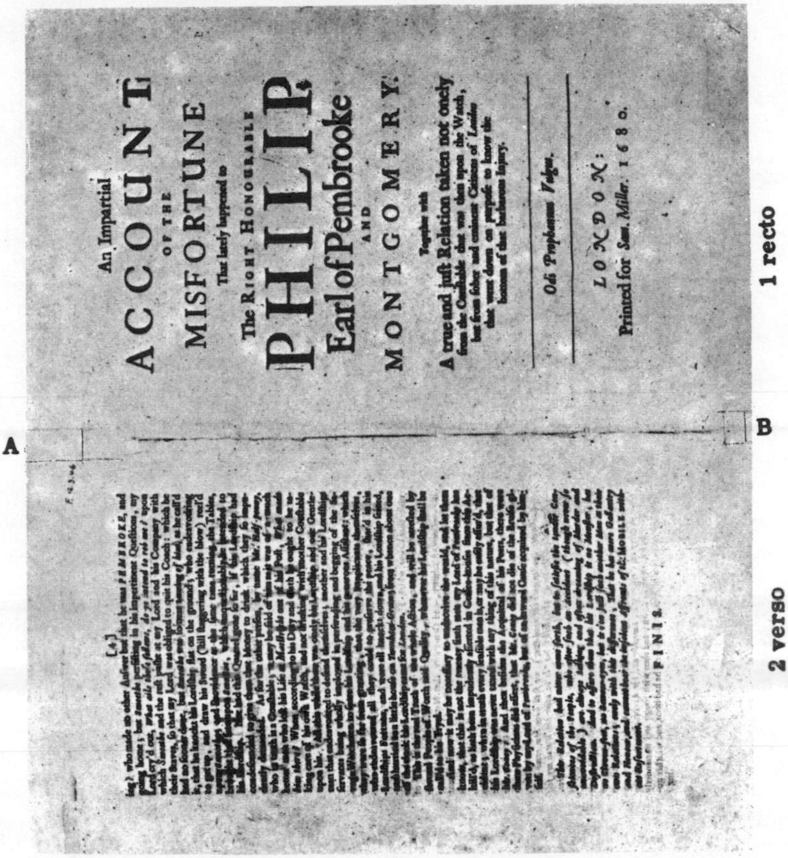

FIG. 4. Folio, outer form. Reproduced, with permission of the Folger Shakespeare Library, Washington, D.C.

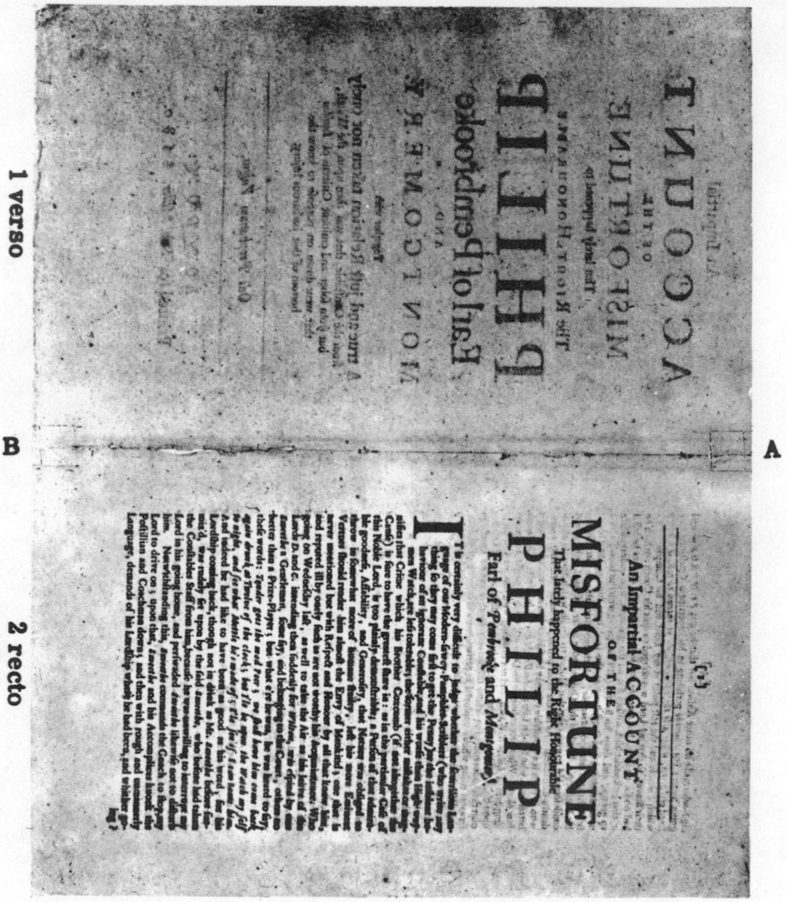

FIG. 5. Folio, inner form. Reproduced, with permission of the Folger Shakespeare Library, Washington, D.C.

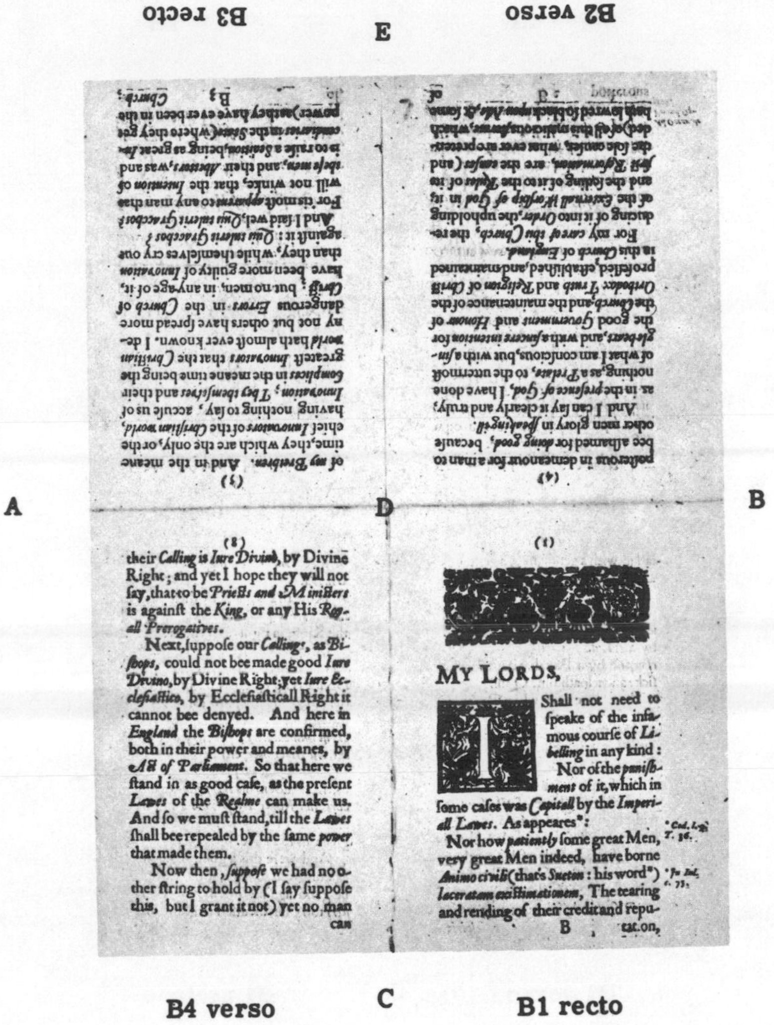

FIG. 6. Quarto, outer form. Reproduced, with permission of the Folger Shakespeare Library, Washington, D.C.

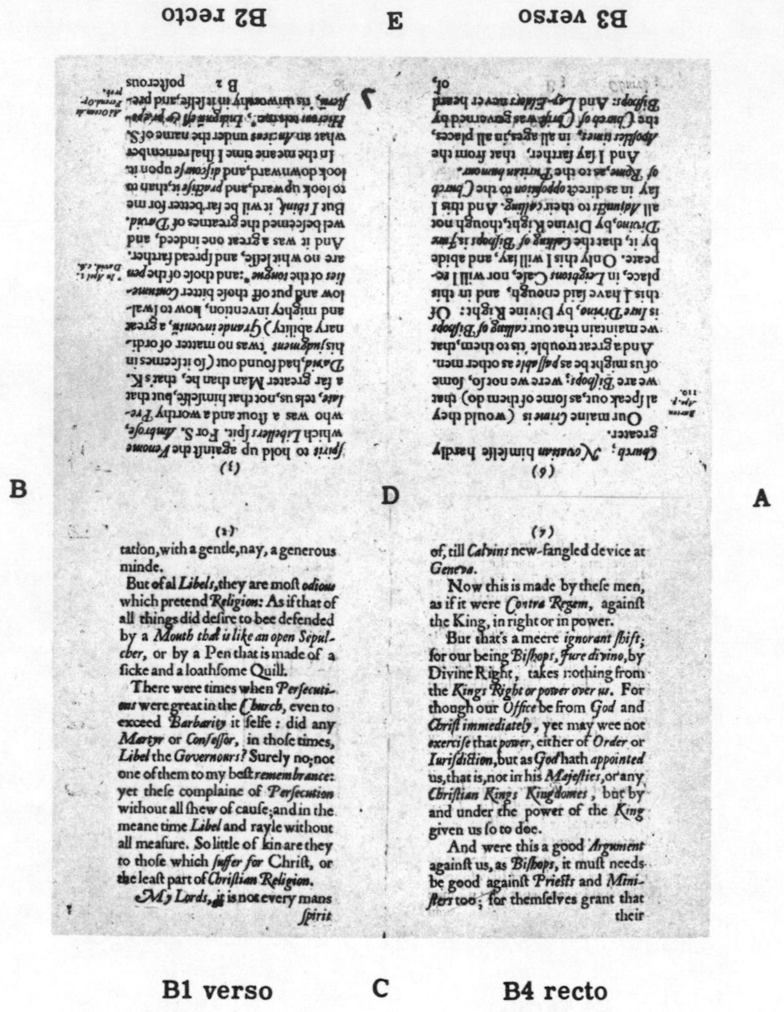

(2)

tation, with a gentle, nay, a generous minde.

But of al *Libels*, they are most *odious* which pretend *Religion*: As if that of all things did desire to bee defended by a *Mouth that is like an open Sepulcher*, or by a Pen that is made of a sicke and a loathsome Quill.

There were times when *Persecutions* were great in the *Church*, even to exceed *Barbarity* it selfe: did any *Martyr* or *Confessor*, in those times, *Libel* the *Governours*? Surely no; not one of them to my best *remembrance*: yet these complaine of *Persecution* without all shew of cause; and in the meane time *Libel* and rayle without all measure. So little of kin are they to those which *suffer for* Christ, or the least part of *Christian Religion*.

My Lords, it is not every mans

spirit

(7)

of, till *Calvins* new-fangled device at *Geneva*.

Now this is made by these men, as if it were *Contra Regem*, against the King, in right or in power.

But that's a meere *ignorant shift*; for our being *Bishops*, *Jure divino*, by Divine Right, takes nothing from the *Kings Right or power over us*. For though our *Office* be from *God* and *Christ immediately*, yet may wee not *exercise* that *power*, either of *Order* or *Iurisdiction*, but as *God* hath *appointed* us, that is, not in his *Majesties*, or any *Christian Kings Kingdomes*, but by and under the power of the *King* given us so to doe.

And were this a good *Argument* against us, as *Bishops*, it must needs be good against *Priests* and *Ministers* too; for themselves grant that

their

FIG. 7. Quarto, inner form. Reproduced, with permission of the Folger Shakespeare Library, Washington, D.C.

line CD, bringing the fold ED inside CD. This results in four leaves after the top folds AD and BD have been cut open. The outer form of the sheet (fig. 6) consists of 1 recto, 2 verso, 3 recto, and 4 verso; and the inner form (fig. 7) consists of 1 verso, 2 recto, 3 verso, and 4 recto. The two outer leaves and the two inner leaves are each conjugate. The catchwords appear at the bottom of each page.

At the bottom of the recto of each of the first three leaves in the gathering is what is called a "signature": B, B2, and B3. The letter B indicates the place of this particular gathering in the book. Gatherings in early books, and in many modern books as well, are arranged in alphabetical sequence; this gathering, for instance, is preceded by a gathering A and followed by a gathering C. Signatures occur only on the rectos of leaves. Generally, only the leaves in the first half of the gathering or, as in this case, the leaves in the first half and the first leaf in the second half are signed. This is particularly true of books printed before 1800; in more recent times it has become customary to sign only the first leaf of each gathering.

The leaves of this gathering may be referred to as B1, B2, B3, and B4; the pages as B1 recto, B1 verso, B2 recto, B2 verso, B3 recto, B3 verso, B4 recto, B4 verso. There seems to be no need actually to use the word "signature"—e.g., "signature B1 recto" or "sig. B1 recto"—although it is sometimes done. Pages or leaves which are not actually signed—e.g., B1 verso or B4—need not be placed within brackets (thus "[B] 1 verso" and "[B4]") because, although they are not signed, they are none the less integral parts of gathering B. The words "recto" and "verso" are usually abbreviated: "A1r" for "A1 recto," for instance, and "A1v" for "A1 verso." On the catalog card the full words may be more readily understood. There is some tendency to omit "recto" (or "r") if it is clear from the context that reference is to only the top page of a leaf. This would mean that, say, "B3" could mean both the third leaf of gathering B and the top page of the third leaf of gathering B; the cataloger has no need for such ambiguity.

There is a great deal of variety in signatures. In Foxe's *Actes and Monuments,* noted earlier, a folio, only the first four leaves in all gatherings of six are signed, but all leaves are signed in most gatherings of four; this is true of four-leaf gatherings in a number of other books printed by John Day. Robert Waldegrave used only numerals on all signed leaves except the first; he would have signed the gathering illustrated thus: B, 2,3. Numerals instead of letters mark gathering sequence in many books, even incunabula; the third volume of Augustine's *Explanatio Psalmorum* (Basel: J. Amerbach, 1489), for instance, is signed throughout with numerals. The practice became quite common in the nineteenth and twentieth centuries. In many modern books each gathering is marked on the edge of the outside fold in such a way that when the gatherings are arranged in proper sequence, the marks (called "back marks") will form a diagonal line across the spine of the book. This row of back marks is concealed entirely when the book is bound. Gatherings of many incunabula are not signed in any way, and occasional unsigned gatherings occur in books of all periods. In the eighteenth century a small arabic figure often was printed at the bottom of a verso page in a form to indicate the press which had run it off; these "press numbers" are not to be confused with signatures.

Sometimes the first leaf of a gathering bears, in addition to the signature, an abbreviation of the title or the volume number of the book—e.g., "Vol.III.A." This, of course, prevented the sheets of one book from being mixed with those of another. On the last leaf of the final volume of Thomas Percy's *Reliques of Ancient English Poetry* (London: Printed for J. Dodsley, 1765) is a printed note to the binder that the sheets of the first and third volumes are wrongly marked; those marked "Vol. I." are to be bound as Volume 3 and those marked "Vol. III." are to be bound as Volume 1. Possibly the copy for Volume 3 came to the printer first and he printed it as Volume 1 before he realized what it was.

In the sheet illustrated (fig. 6) the chain lines run parallel to the fold AB, and there is a watermark in the center of the B2–B3 half. One chain line, for instance, passes through B4 verso at "Now" (line 19) and continues in B1 recto through "Animo" (line 12). The watermark may be seen in the original on B2 verso touching "maintained" (line 12) and extending down to "the re-" (line 14); it goes across the fold DE and in B3 recto extends from "have been" (line 12) down to "against it" (line 14).

So in a 4to leaf the chain lines are horizontal, and the chain lines of two conjugate 4to leaves meet at the fold. In a 4to gathering of four leaves, 1 and 2 are conjugate with 4 and 3 and their chain lines meet. If there is a watermark centrally placed in one half of the sheet, it shows in the middle inner fold of leaves 1 and 4 or 2 and 3. If the watermark is small or slightly off center, it may show in only one of two conjugate 4to leaves.

The 4to gathering was popular in the sixteenth and seventeenth centuries. Although a 4to gathering in four leaves is usual, there are also 4to gatherings of two, six, eight, or even ten or more leaves. An eight-leaf 4to gathering results when two complete sheets printed in 4to are folded and then placed one inside the other. In such a gathering leaves 1 and 2 are conjugate with 8 and 7, while leaves 3 and 4 are conjugate with 6 and 5, because each set of four leaves resulted when a sheet was folded into four. A 4to gathering of two, six, or ten leaves generally comes as the final gathering of a book composed of four- or eight-leaf gatherings if the text remaining is not quite enough, or is more than enough, to occupy a gathering of normal size.

A 4to gathering of two leaves results when one half of a sheet is folded by itself, and a gathering of six leaves results if such a half sheet is placed inside (or sometimes outside) a sheet folded into four in the normal way. A ten-leaf gathering is formed if such a half sheet is placed inside (or sometimes between or outside) two sheets each of which has been folded into four in the normal way. In a 4to gathering of two leaves, 1 and 2 are conjugate; in a six-leaf gathering, 1, 2, and 3 are conjugate with 6,

5, and 4; and in a ten-leaf gathering, 1, 2, 3, 4, and 5 are conjugate with 10, 9, 8, 7, and 6.

Octavos

The octavo (8vo) gathering in eight leaves (figs. 8 and 9) is from an almanac by Nostradamus for 1562. The sheet is folded along line AB and then along line CD, bringing the fold ED inside CD. (Thus far the folding is the same as for a 4to.) The sheet is then folded once more along line FG, bringing the fold HI inside FG, the fold IK inside HI, and the fold LG inside IK. This produces eight separate leaves after their top folds CG, GD, DI, and IE and their two outer folds AD and DB have been opened. A1, A2, A3, and A4 are then conjugate with only A8, A7, A6, and A5. The outer form (fig. 8) consists of A1 recto, A2 verso, A3 recto, A4 verso, A5 recto, A6 verso, A7 recto, and A8 verso; the inner form (fig. 9), of A1 verso, A2 recto, A3 verso, A4 recto, A5 verso, A6 recto, A7 verso, and A8 recto. No catchwords were used for this particular book; this is unusual for the period. Also, it will be noted that only A3 recto is signed; it is usual for the first five rectos in such a gathering to be signed.

The chain lines run parallel to the main fold AB and the inner folds FG, GL, HI, and IK. This means that in each leaf the chain lines are vertical and that for this reason they cannot meet at the inner fold with the chain lines of a conjugate leaf—e.g., the chain lines of A1 and A8 are vertical and parallel, instead of meeting at the inner fold as they would in two conjugate 4to leaves. Instead, the chain lines of A1 cross the top fold CG and enter A4, and the chain lines of A8 cross the top fold GD and enter A5. In the same way the chain lines of A7 and A2 meet those of A6 and A3 at the top folds DI and IE. In an 8vo gathering of eight leaves, then, the chain lines are vertical in each leaf and they meet at the top edges of leaves 1 and 4, 2 and 3, 5 and 8, and 6 and 7. This is true even if the top edges have been trimmed unmercifully.

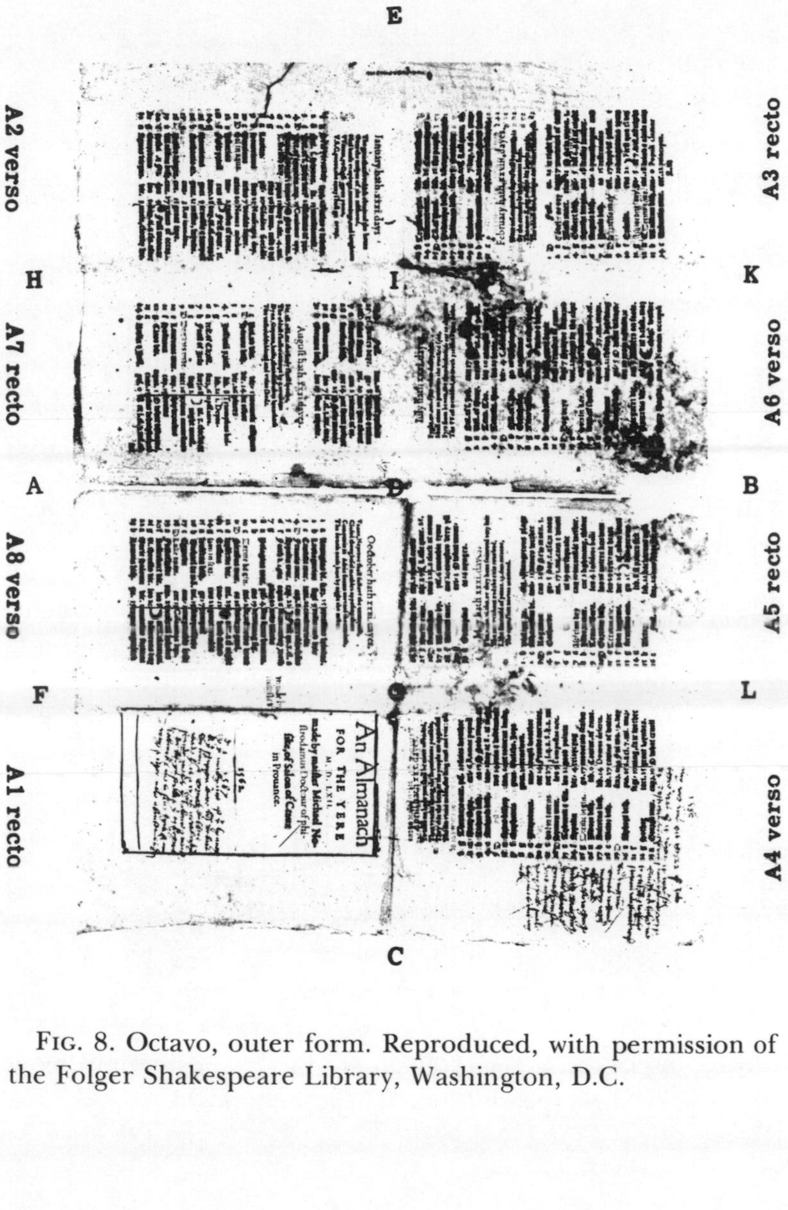

FIG. 8. Octavo, outer form. Reproduced, with permission of the Folger Shakespeare Library, Washington, D.C.

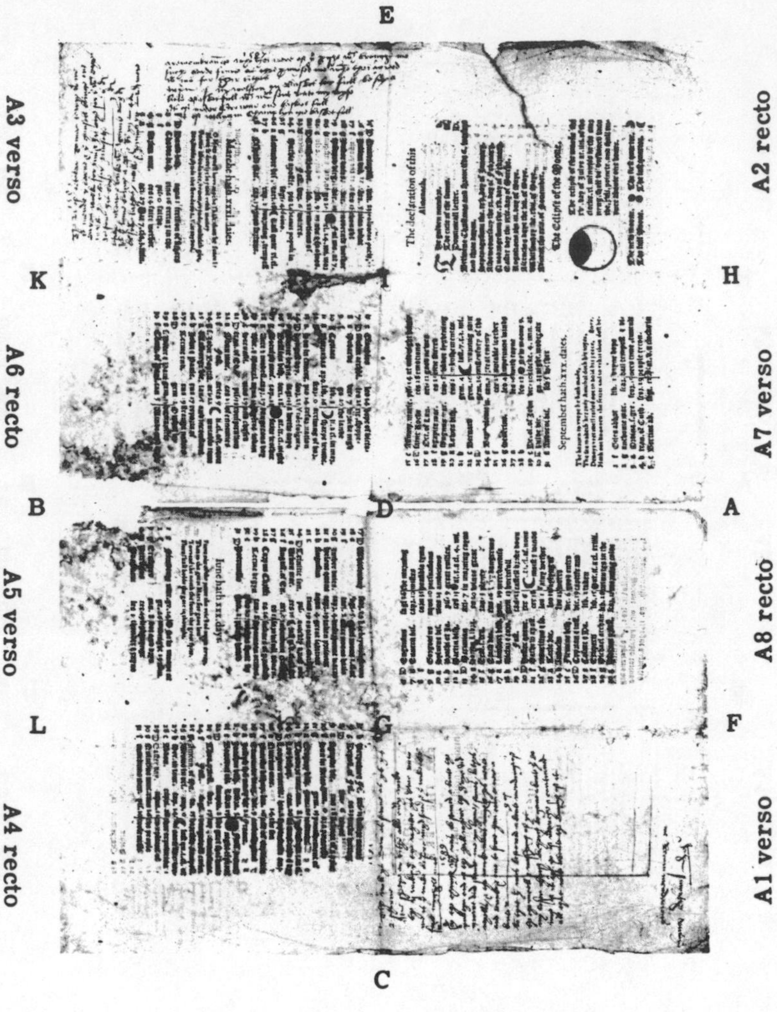

FIG. 9. Octavo, inner form. Reproduced, with permission of the Folger Shakespeare Library, Washington, D.C.

There is no watermark in the 8vo sheet illustrated. If there is a watermark in the exact center of one half of an 8vo sheet and if it is so large that it is not cut away when the book is trimmed, then each of the four leaves in that half (1, 8, 4, and 5 or 2, 7, 3, and 6) has in its upper inner margin a fragment of a watermark which meets at the inner fold (FG and GL or HI and IK) with the watermark fragment of the leaf with which it is conjugate and at the top edge (CG and GD or DI and IE) with the watermark fragment in the leaf whose chain lines it matches. Actually the watermark is often neither large nor placed in the exact center of one half of the sheet. In that case it generally appears in at least two leaves of the half sheet—i.e., two leaves which are conjugate or whose chain lines match at the top edges. Occasionally it is so small and so much off center that it appears in only one leaf in the gathering.

During the eighteenth century the 8vo gathering of four leaves was popular. Such a gathering is formed from one half of a sheet. Leaves 1 and 2 are conjugate with 4 and 3, and chain lines and watermark (if there is one) in 1 and 4 meet those of 2 and 3 at their top margins.

There are also 8vo gatherings of two leaves, six leaves, ten leaves and sometimes more. The two-leaf gathering may be formed by cutting away any two conjugate leaves in a sheet printed in 8vo; chain lines are, of course, vertical and unless you can actually *see* where the two leaves join, you can never be certain that they are conjugate. The six-leaf gathering is what remains after one pair of conjugate leaves has been cut out of an 8vo sheet. The chain lines and possibly the watermark in one pair of conjugate leaves meet those of another pair at the top margins, but the third pair of conjugate leaves has chain lines and possibly watermark in common only with the pair of leaves which has been removed. A ten-leaf 8vo gathering results when two conjugate 8vo leaves are placed inside or outside an 8vo gathering of eight leaves; chain lines and watermark tell you which leaves belong to the eight-leaf gathering.

Twelvemos

The duodecimo or "twelvemo" (12mo) gathering of twelve leaves may be produced by folding the sheet in one of at least two different ways: (1) individual leaves in the sheet may be so arranged that the sheet has to be cut once before it can be folded (figs. 10 and 11), or (2) they may be so arranged that the sheet can be folded without cutting (figs. 12 and 13). The first method appears to have been almost the only one used prior to about 1800.

After printing, the sheet is cut along line XZ (fig. 10). Then the two-thirds section is folded along line AB and again along line CD, bringing the fold ED inside CD. (Thus far the folding is the same as for a 4to.) The section is folded once more along line FG, bringing the fold HI inside FG, IK inside HI, and LG inside IK. (The folding of the two-thirds section is thus the same as for an 8vo.) The one-third section is folded along BN and then along line KO, bringing the fold LM inside KO. The folded one-third section is placed inside the folded two-thirds section. The outside fold of the entire gathering is along line FG, and inside it are folds in the following order: HI, IK, LG, KO, and LM. This results in twelve separate leaves after the top folds CG, GD, DI, and IE and the outer folds AD, DB, and BN have been opened. A1, A2, A3, A4, A5, and A6 are conjugate with A12, A11, A10, A9, A8, and A7. The outer form (fig. 10) consists of: A1 recto, A2 verso, A3 recto, A4 verso, A5 recto, A6 verso, A7 recto, A8 verso, A9 recto, A10 verso, A11 recto, and A12 verso. The inner form (fig. 11) consists of: A1 verso, A2 recto, A3 verso, A4 recto, A5 verso, A6 recto, A7 verso, A8 recto, A9 verso, A10 recto, A11 verso, and A12 recto.

Chain lines in the sheet are parallel to lines CE and XZ. Chain lines in each leaf are, therefore, horizontal, and in each pair of conjugate leaves chain lines meet at the inner fold: A1 and A12 at FG, A2 and A11 at HI, A3 and A10 at IK, A4 and A9 at GL, A5 and A8 at KO, and A6 and A7 at LM. In addition, the chain lines of two consecutive leaves with a common outer fold meet at that outer fold (or at their outer edges if the fold has

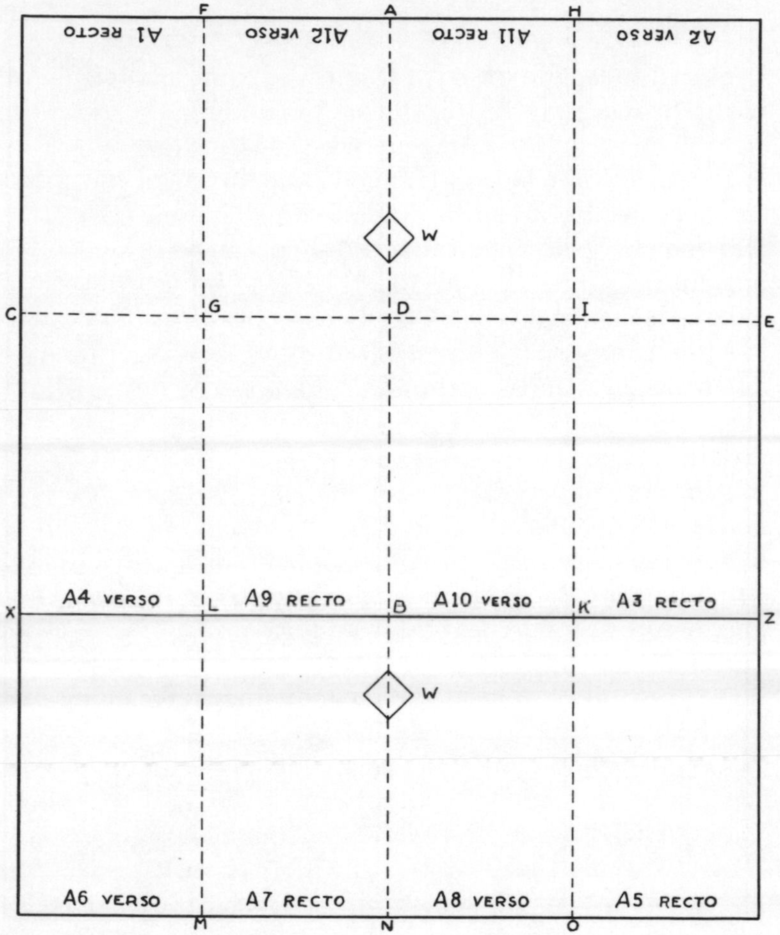

FIG. 10. Twelvemo by cutting, outer form

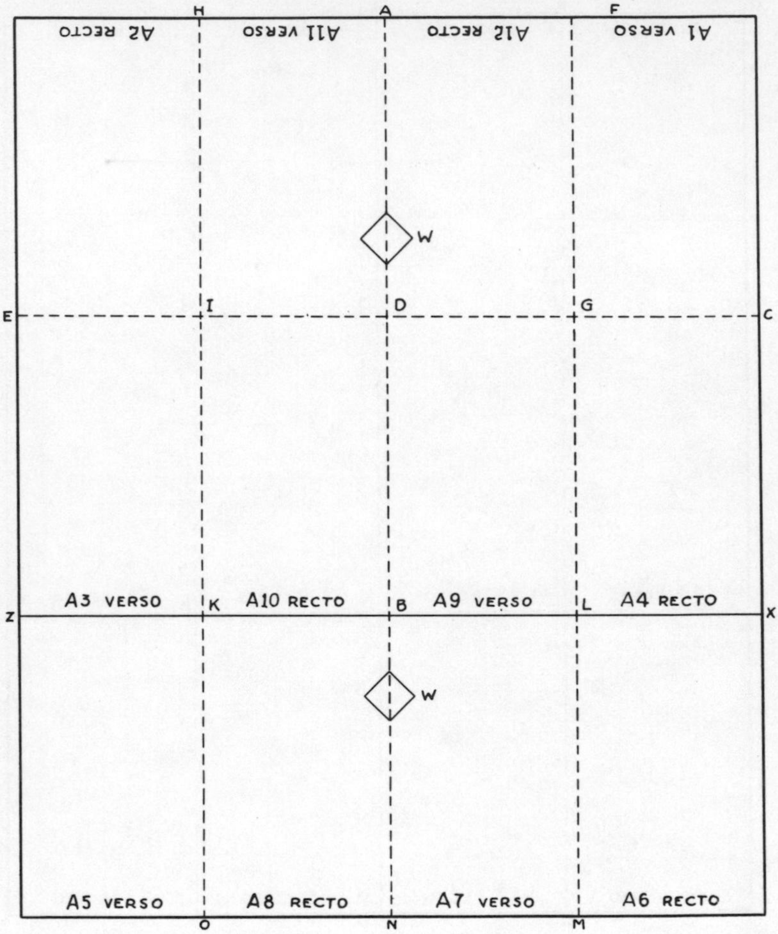

FIG. 11. Twelvemo by cutting, inner form

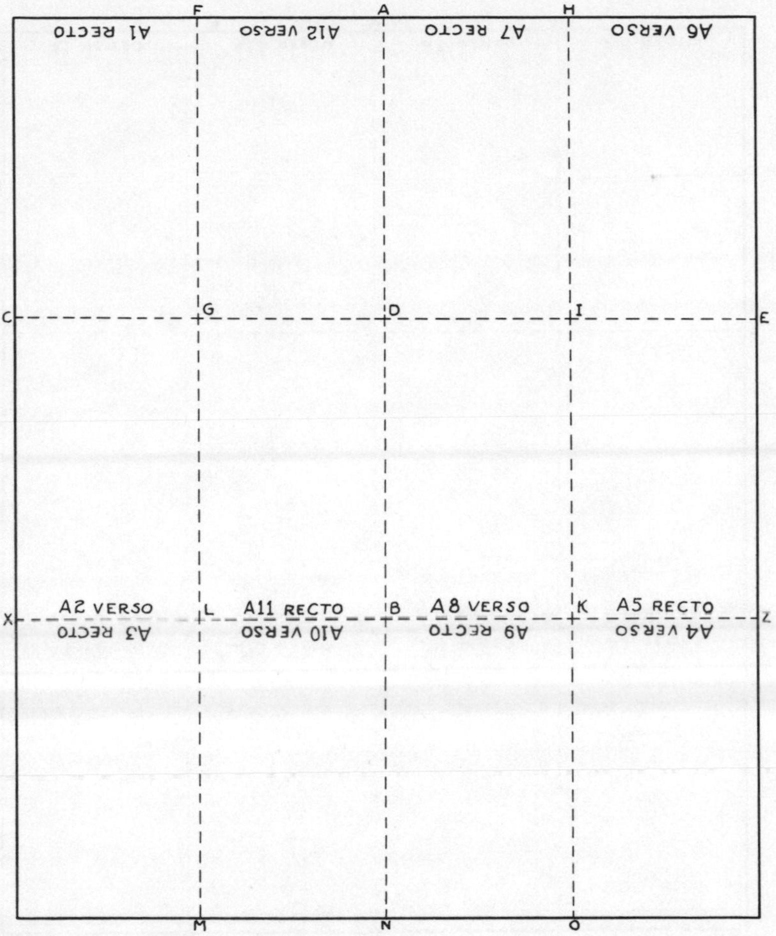

FIG. 12. Twelvemo without cutting, outer form

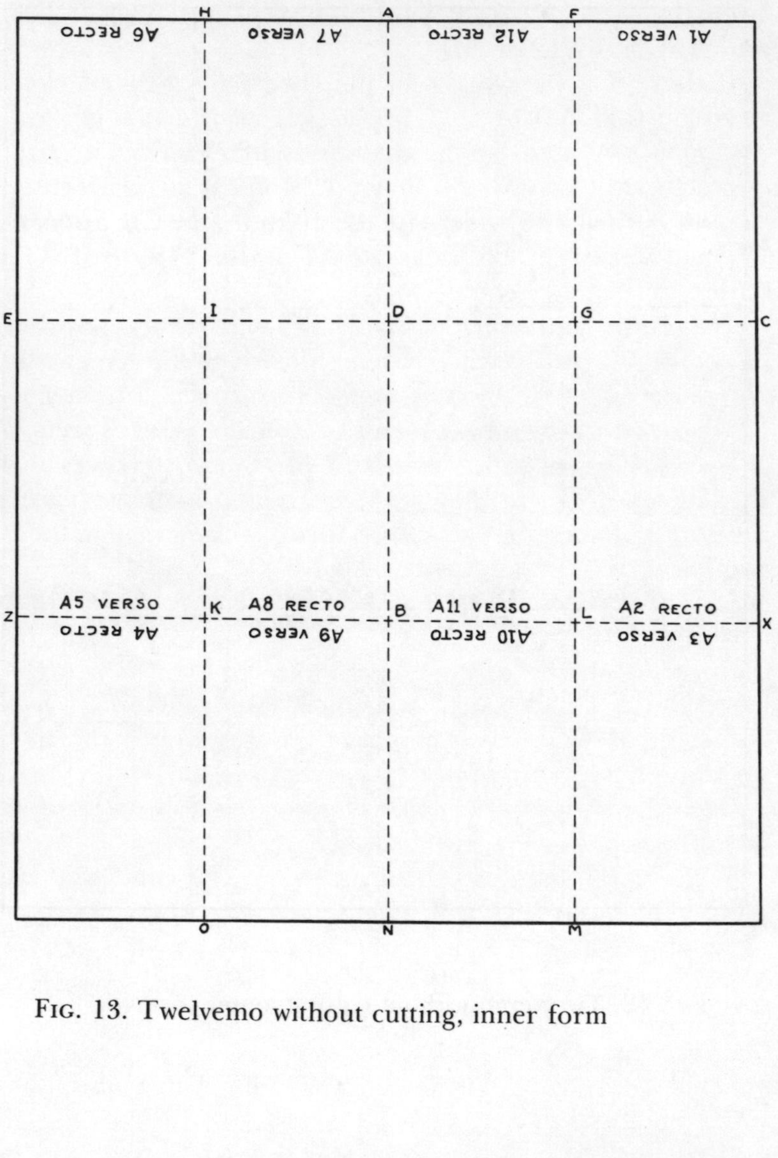

FIG. 13. Twelvemo without cutting, inner form

been opened): A7 and A8 at BN, A9 and A10 at DB, and A11 and A12 at AD.

If there is a watermark in the sheet, it is located close to or on fold AD or fold BN in one of the two general positions indicated by the diamonds marked W. Its size, of course, will vary, and it may not be in the precise center of one half of the sheet. In the folded sheet it appears in the outer edge (or edges) of A7 and/or A8 or of A11 and/or A12.

The 12mo gathering of six leaves was rather popular in the eighteenth century. After printing, the sheet was cut along line AN, dividing it into two halves. The halves were also cut along lines XB and BZ. The two-thirds section of each half was then folded (like a 4to) into four leaves and the one-third section into two leaves which could be placed inside the four-leaf part, thus forming from each sheet two gatherings of six leaves each.

Also common are 12mo gatherings of four and of eight leaves. A gathering of eight leaves is produced simply by folding two-thirds of the sheet (like an 8vo) into eight leaves. Such a gathering can be distinguished from an 8vo gathering of eight leaves because (1) it is usually somewhat smaller, (2) it has horizontal (instead of vertical) chain lines, and (3) the watermark is in the outer (instead of the top inner) margin.

A 12mo gathering of four leaves may be produced by folding one third of the sheet along line BN and then along line KO. Such a gathering, like a regular 4to gathering of four leaves, has horizontal chain lines. However, it can be distinguished from the 4to because (1) it is smaller, (2) if there is a watermark, it appears in the outer margins of leaves 3 and 4 instead of in the inner margins of 1 and 4 or 2 and 3, and (3) the chain lines of leaves 3 and 4 meet in their outer margins (in the 4to gathering no chain lines have to meet in outer margins). It would be possible also to get a four-leaf gathering from half of a two-thirds section of a 12mo sheet. If the two thirds section were cut along line AB, each of the resulting halves could be folded into four, one along line CD and then along

FG, and the other along DE and then HI. Such a gathering could be distinguished from a regular 4to gathering in four leaves because it would be smaller and the watermark (if there were one) would appear in the outer, instead of the inner, margins.

The 12mo without cutting (figs. 12 and 13) came into use in the nineteenth century. The top and bottom thirds of the sheet are folded along lines CE and XZ in opposite directions (z-fashion), in such a way that when the sheet is then folded along line AD, the fold DB comes within AD and the fold BN within DB. The sheet is folded once more along line FG, and inside FG will be folds in this order: GL, LM, OK, KI, and IH. Much nineteenth-century paper has no chain lines. If there are chain lines in a 12mo without cutting, they are, of course, horizontal in individual leaves and they meet in the outer margins of 7 and 12, 8 and 11, and 9 and 10, as well as at the inner margins of each pair of conjugate leaves.

FOLIO, QUARTO, OCTAVO, AND TWELVEMO

If the book is	Each sheet folds into a gathering of	In which chain lines are	And chain lines meet
folio (fo)	2 leaves	vertical	nowhere
quarto (4to)	4 leaves	horizontal	at inner margins of leaves 1 & 4; 2 & 3
octavo (8vo)	8 leaves	vertical	at top margins of leaves 1 & 4; 2 & 3; 5 & 8; 6 & 7
twelvemo (12mo) by cutting	12 leaves	horizontal	at inner margins of leaves 1 & 12; 2 & 11; 3 & 10; 4 & 9; 5 & 8; 6 & 7 and at outer margins of leaves 7 & 8; 9 & 10; 11 & 12

Smaller Formats

Most books printed prior to 1800, and many printed since then, are composed of gatherings folded into folio, 4to, 8vo, or 12mo leaves according to the schemes just outlined. More leaves can be secured from a sheet merely by folding the sheet more times than are required for the traditional schemes; this produces leaves in 16mo, 18mo, 24mo, 32mo, and other smaller sizes. A gathering of more than eight or twelve leaves, however, has a thick fold; such a fold is hard for the binder to sew and causes a book to bulge at the spine. For this reason, 16mo and 32mo leaves are often in gatherings of eight or even four leaves, and 24mo in twelve or six. So long as the sheet remained small, these more complicated foldings were used only when a very small book was desired.

As the size of the sheet increased, so also the size of the leaf increased. Some eighteenth-century quartos are as large as early seventeenth-century folios. Beginning in the eighteenth century, and perhaps somewhat earlier, the complicated foldings became more popular because the leaves they produced were large enough for ordinary books. Also printers sometimes cut large sheets in half and then printed and folded these half sheets by one of the four traditional schemes, as though they were whole sheets; this, of course, resulted in folio and 8vo leaves with horizontal chain lines and 4to and 12mo leaves with vertical chain lines—unless, indeed, one wishes to consider leaves so printed as 4to, 16mo, 8vo, and 24mo.

Chain lines in a 16mo leaf are horizontal, meeting at the inner fold with those of a conjugate leaf. In a 16mo gathering of eight leaves the chain lines (and watermark fragments if there are any) of leaves 5 and 7 meet those of 6 and 8 in the outer margins.

In a 32mo leaf the chain lines are vertical; and in a 32mo gathering of eight leaves they match at the top margins as in an 8vo gathering of eight leaves—i.e., 1 and 4, 2 and 3, 5 and 8, 6 and 7—but the leaves are smaller than 8vo and the watermark, when present, is in the lower outside margin.

An 18mo leaf has vertical chain lines; in an 18mo gathering of six leaves the chain lines of leaves 1 and 6 meet those of 2 and 5 at the top margins, and the chain lines at the bottom margin of leaves 2 and 5 match those at the top margin of 3 and 4.

The chain lines of a 24mo are vertical if one of the two 12mo foldings described above is again folded; it is possible, however, for a 24mo leaf to have horizontal chain lines.

Because leaves smaller than 12mo generally appear in gatherings formed by folding less than one whole sheet, it is often hard to tell the size of the original sheet and how many leaves came from it. This may safely be left to the experts. About the format of such books no one may reasonably expect the card to tell more than (1) how many leaves there are in each gathering, and (2) whether or not any leaves are lacking or replaced by other leaves. These questions one can readily answer if he remembers that (1) the chain lines in any gathering follow a definite pattern, meeting (except in gatherings of two leaves with vertical chain lines) sometimes at outer margins, sometimes at inner margins, sometimes at both, and that (2) in any book the chain lines of all gatherings of the same number of leaves normally follow the same pattern.

Wove Paper

All European and American books before 1757 were printed on paper containing chain lines. In that year appeared John Baskerville's *Virgil,* in which "wove" paper was used for the first time. Wove paper was made in molds with bottoms of closely woven brass wire, and for that reason it had neither chain lines nor wire lines. By the 1790s wove paper was quite common. The woven wire principle was carried over into the papermaking machines developed in the nineteenth century, although there has always been, of course, some handmade chain line paper, and chain line designs are sometimes artificially added to machine-made wove paper.

With wove paper it is impossible to tell whether or not

one leaf is conjugate with another unless you can actually see where they join, and if the paper has been trimmed, you have no way of telling the size of the original sheet or how many times it has been folded. Fortunately the publisher's cloth case binding came into vogue during the 1820s; and because the original binding thus became part of the book as issued, collectors have tended to keep it intact. For this reason the first edition of a nineteenth- or twentieth-century book is much more apt than an early book to have its leaves still untrimmed and sometimes even unopened. Moreover, cloth cases are looser than leather bindings. The cataloger will find it relatively easy to see the sewing thread at the center of the gathering, and probably he can even see where each leaf joins another at the fold. If the leaves have not been opened, he can see how the original sheet was folded; and if they have been opened with a paper knife, he may still be able to match jagged edges.

Made-Up Copies

A made-up copy results when a binder and/or former owner attempts to restore the imperfection(s) of a book with leaves or gatherings in pen and ink facsimile, from another copy, edition, or issue of the book, or from some other source. Pen and ink facsimile is generally quite easy to detect; and other kinds of made-up copies sometimes have telltale features. Sometimes the feel of the paper or the size or style of the type betrays the insert. Sometimes the leaf or gathering is taken from another copy or edition which has been trimmed somewhat more (or less) than the book in which it is inserted. Sometimes the edges of the book or the insert have been gilded and the others have not. Sometimes there are wormholes or stains which go through the book but do not appear in (say) gathering G; sometimes the reverse is true. Sometimes the chain lines are farther apart (or closer together) than in the paper of the rest of the book. Sometimes the headlines are differently phrased or in different size or style of type. If only one leaf is involved, it may be pasted in or attached to a stub and sewed in; if it is attached to another leaf, chain lines will not match.

Occasionally the former owner or the binder has written a note in the book telling what he has done; generally the cataloger will have to find the evidence himself. Speaking broadly, a made-up copy is apt to be a copy of a very rare book and/or handsomely bound.

Examination

The examination of a book is nothing more than the examination of a series of gatherings. As the cataloger turns the leaves, he will want to make sure that: (1) the signatures follow in proper sequence and no leaf is signed differently from other leaves in the book; (2) every catchword at the lower inner margin matches the first word of the next page; (3) each gathering has its full share of leaves; (4) no leaf is attached to a stub instead of to another leaf; and (5) everything looks as if it belonged. An unusual signature or an unmatched catchword may be only a printer's error; a gathering with more or fewer leaves than usual may be what the text required; a leaf attached to a stub may be a one-leaf engraving; and something which looks strange may turn out to belong after all. But such things may also be warning signals which will lead the cataloger to a cancel or facsimile leaf or a leaf or gathering inserted from another copy or edition. He can be sure only if he stops and looks at the chain lines and watermark of the gathering in which they occur and (if possible) sees where each leaf in the gathering actually joins another leaf. He cannot look too closely at leaves of first and last gatherings. They have had the most wear, and they include the title page and often the colophon leaf, the two leaves in the book which a printer is most apt to cancel and a forger to fake.

With practice all this becomes automatic and requires much less time than one might think.

6. The Founder and the Alphabet: Collation

When the College Founder, back in England some three hundred years ago, lugged his closely written manuscript into the printshop, the printer may have gone at once to the case and started setting type. But he would not begin with the title page and immediately plunge into the Founder's detailed explanation to the Bishop of Landsend that he ventured to submit these unworthy offspring of his lowly muse to the candid eye of the learned not from any sense of his own greatness but only because of the continued entreaty of his friends.

The printer would know that his type supply was limited and that when he had set type for one gathering, he would have to print all the necessary copies of that gathering almost immediately so that he could use the type again on later sections of the book. And the text of that gathering, once it had been printed, could not be changed. All copies of the next gathering would have to be printed in turn as soon as set up, and the next, and the next. When he had finally arrived at the Founder's neatly inscribed "Finis," he might find that he had only half a page of text for his last four-leaf gathering. If he still had the title page and dedication to print, he might be able to fill some of those blank leaves at the end with material to be used at the beginning of the book.

Moreover, the printer would be wise in the ways of men or, at least, of authors. He would have no way of knowing that *Sixty Sermons Sauing Sinners' Sicke Soules* would forever ring as music celestial in the Founder's ears; after all there had been an author only last month who changed his title just as the last gathering was going through the press.

Again, the Founder's book would look like a longish job, and the Bishop of Landsend was a mortal man; one does not dedicate books to dead bishops. Or the Bishop of Landsend might be translated to the diocese of Crough, or the Founder might be an overblunt man who would no longer cherish the Bishop when printing was finished. Or the Founder might want to add something. . . .

So the printer would skip the dedication and begin setting type for Sermon 1. He might label the page "1" and at its bottom he would sign the gathering "B," leaving A for the title page and the dedication to the Bishop. He would set the gathering—say a 4to in four leaves with the first three leaves signed "B," "B2," and "B3"—and it would be printed while he went ahead setting type for gathering C and then gathering D, stopping to "distribute" the type (i.e., to return it letter by letter to the case in which it was kept) as the printing of each gathering was finished. His signatures would go through the alphabet, except that there would be no gathering J, no U, and no W. When he came to Z, he would begin again with Aa, Bb, Cc (or AA, BB, CC), and so on to Zz (or ZZ), and then he would begin again with Aaa (or AAA). The days and weeks would slip by and at last he would really come to that "Finis" on the verso of the third leaf in gathering Bbb.

The good Bishop, no doubt a strict vegetarian and a sound sleeper, would have survived the printing of the Founder's opus still hale and hearty, still in the Founder's good graces, and still Bishop of Landsend—the reader may remember (see the third chapter if not) that the Rev. Dr. Heggsby became Bishop of Crough while gathering B was going through the press. So the dedication could now be set and printed. It would make six pages (three leaves) and with the title leaf would exactly fill gathering A.

Collation: Definition

The number of gatherings in a book and the number of leaves in each gathering make up the "collation" of the book. Collation may also be given by pages or leaves, but collation by gatherings is more useful because a book is an orderly group of gatherings, not a mere collection of pages or leaves.

For this reason many wrong page or leaf numbers occur in early books but seldom any really misleading signatures or catchwords. Both the printer and the binder needed signatures and catchwords to arrange the leaves within the gathering and the gatherings within the book. Leaf numbers ("foliation") and (in later books) page numbers were added as an afterthought for possible convenience of the reader. Only in the late eighteenth century did page numbers begin to displace signatures and catchwords as aids in the arrangement of leaves within a gathering. Even today most gatherings are signed in some way, and the gathering is still the fundamental unit of the physical book.

Because a rare book is valuable chiefly, if not only, as a physical entity, the description of a rare book must make the book's physical structure perfectly clear.

Collation of an ordinary book is given only by pages. This is as it should be; the prospective user of that book wants to know only what it is about and how much of it there is for him to read. At the same time this means that most of the people who look at the catalog card for the *Sermons* are accustomed only to collation by pages. So the set of gatherings must be described in the simplest way.

Collation: Statement

The gatherings of the Founder's book might be described as follows:

> A-Z each 4 leaves, Aa-Zz each 4 leaves, Aaa-Bbb each 4 leaves,

or

> A-Z in 4's, Aa-Zz in 4's, Aaa-Bbb in 4's.

But the statement of collation need not be so clumsy

or repetitious. For instance, when the printer began a new two-letter alphabet with Aa after gathering Z, and a three-letter alphabet with Aaa after Zz, he was simply following a practice observed in most books with alphabetical signatures. To the printer and to the user of a book it is as normal to move from Z to Aa and from Zz to Aaa as it is to move from A to B or to omit J, U, and W. So the collation of the *Sermons* would be readily understood if it ran:

A-Bbb each 4 leaves

or

A-Bbb in 4's.

Signatures such as Bbb can be represented simply as "3B." Thus, when a signature runs into a large number of letters, the statement of collation gains greatly in simplicity and (frequently) accuracy as well as space. The last letter signature in Willem Sewel's *History of the . . . Quakers* (3d ed., cor. Philadelphia: S. Keimer, 1728)—a book whose last portion was printed by young Ben Franklin and Hugh Meredith in their newly established printshop—is Sfsssss. This can be represented as "7S."

It is true that "3B" could mean either Bbb or BBB, but this distinction is seldom worth preserving, any more than it is worthwhile to record which leaves are signed in black letter, which in italic, and which in roman. The printer used black letter, for instance, for one signature merely because he happened to be setting a line or two of the text which required black letter when he came to the end of the page and he was standing nearer the black letter case than the roman. Likewise he signed it Bbb instead of BBB merely from personal preference or habit. Usually he sought to distinguish one gathering from another by the letter rather than the type with which he signed it, and one signature sequence from another by the number rather than the kind of letters.

The cataloger may, indeed, take it as a general principle in giving collation that he needs to record only those aspects of a signature which are necessary to set it off from all other signatures in the book.

Occasionally there are signature sequences which cannot be compressed in this manner because the printer did distinguish them by kind, as well as by number, of letters employed. The second volume of Richard Grafton's *Chronicle* (London: Printed by H. Denham for R. Tottle and H. Toye, 1569) has signatures A-Y, Aa-Yy, Aaa-Yyy, Aaaa-Yyyy, and so on; and Hugh Latimer's *Frutefull Sermons* (London: J. Day, 1578) has sequences beginning A, Aa, and AA; such signatures would need to be copied in full. John Foxe's *Actes and Monuments* (London: J. Day, 1570) has sequences beginning A, Aa, AA, AAa, AAA, AAAa, AAAA, AAAAa, and AAAAA; these may be shortened conveniently: "A, Aa, 2A, 2Aa, 3A, 3Aa, 4A, 4Aa, and 5A," but no sequence can very well be omitted in the statement of collation. The first volume of Pierre Bayle's *Dictionary* (2d ed.; London: Printed for J. J. and P. Knapton [etc.], 1734) has sequences beginning A, Aa, Aaa, Aaaa, 5A, 6A, 7A, 8A, 9A; such a series could be represented as "A-9A" with a note within parentheses immediately following the collation: "Gatherings 5A-9A are actually so signed." Augustine's *De Civitate Dei* (Lowen: J. von Paderborn, 1488), a folio, has sequences beginning a and A, and such sequences are found frequently in quite early books. But in later books lower-case letters are only now and then used to sign a few gatherings, generally preliminary or interpolated. For this reason a statement of the signatures in the Augustine probably should run "a-z, A-P" instead of "a-P."

It is convenient to represent the number of leaves in each gathering by a superior number, thus: "A-G^4" rather than "A-G, each four leaves" or "A-G in 4's." The superior figure is, of course, an arbitrary symbol which has no necessary connection with the printing process or the book. But this symbol, unlike those invented by Greg and Bowers, is traditional; like the word "gathering" itself, the superior figure is part of the basic language spoken by all students of rare books. Even if the user of the card is unfamiliar with it, he can easily guess its meaning if he looks into the book. So the collation of the *Sermons* may run simply: "A-3B^4."

Collation, it may be noted, describes the book as issued, not as printed. It is often difficult to determine the order in which gatherings were printed, and it would be equally difficult to represent that order adequately. So in the collation of the Founder's *Sermons* gathering A comes first, although it was actually printed last.

Insertions

Just as the last copy of gathering A came from the press, the Founder may have burst in with a beaming smile and more copy. Perhaps an Oxford dean had dashed off sixty elegiac distichs in elegant Latin—all things were possible in that distant day—one distich to praise each sermon; they simply *had* to come after the dedication. And the Founder himself may have recalled only now the words of that eloquent, but unfortunately extempore, peroration on the fires of damnation which had so moved Sir Theophilus Buzbe, Bart., when Sermon 30 was delivered—couldn't that be worked in somehow?

The printer might think a thing or two about the fires of damnation himself, but he would look over the copy: about four pages (two leaves) for the Latin and, if he crowded it, four pages (two leaves more) for the Founder's eloquence. Lucky that Sermon 30 as now printed ended at the very bottom of Bb3 verso! He would set up and print off the additions as a 4to sheet of four leaves and then cut the sheet to fold into two gatherings of two leaves each. The first leaf of the Dean's distichs he might sign "*" and the Founder's fires he might leave unsigned.

The collation of the *Sermons* could now be written:

> A^4, *^{2}, B-2A^4, 2B^4 (+ a 2-leaf unsigned gathering after 2B3), 2C-3B^4.

or

> A^4, *^{2}, B-2A^4, 2B^6 (2B1, 2B2, and 2B4 are conjugate with 2B6, 2B3, and 2B5), 2C-3B^4.

or

A-3B^4 (+ two 2-leaf gatherings: one, signed *, after A4, and another, unsigned, after 2B3).

The first statement is probably preferable. It is clearer than the second because it describes the book entirely in terms of gatherings: 2B is not one but two gatherings, and to call it otherwise is to force the facts. This distinction is not simply pedantic, because the reader of the first statement knows at once that the unsigned gathering was an afterthought. The first statement is more graphic than the third because it interrupts the collation to explain each abnormal situation at the very place where the reader will find it as he turns the leaves of the book. But the cataloger will come across some unusual gatherings which he can describe only by formulas such as the second or third.

If the first or the third statement is used, the first leaf of the inserted gathering may be referred to as "2B3+1" and the second leaf as "2B3+2." Leaves in gathering * would of course be "*1" and "*2."

Issues

Different issues of a book generally have somewhat different collations. Another issue of the *Sermons* would have resulted if the Founder had later brought in a sixty-first sermon and if it had been printed and bound with the unsold copies of the book. The additional gatherings would probably be signed in the sequence already begun and might continue through Fff. For this issue the final section of the collation would read not "2C-3B^4" but "2C-3F^4."

Cancels often distinguish issues. In one issue of the *Sermons* the leaf containing pages 3-4 (B2) might be a cancel replacing a leaf on which Bishop Heggsby's name had been misprinted "Hoggsty." The collation of such an issue would begin: A^4, *^{2}, B^4 (B2 is a cancel), C-2A^4, and so on.

The book might be handled by two booksellers (call them Black and Blue), each of whom insisted that the title page name him only. If the printer knew of this circumstance before he printed gathering A, which contained the title page A1, he would first set up the imprint for, say, Black. As soon as he had printed enough copies of gathering A to go with the batch of books Black expected to sell, he would stop the press and change the imprint name to "Blue" before he printed the remaining copies of gathering A. In this case, both the Black issue and the Blue issue would have the collation as given above:

A^4, $*^2$, and so on.

But if Blue came on the scene only after all copies of gathering A had been printed naming Black, then the printer would have to set up and print a cancel title page naming Blue, and the Blue issue would have the collation:

A^4 (A1 is a cancel), $*^2$, and so on.

Fifteen years later the bookseller Green (no doubt he bought out Black and Blue) might still have some unsold copies of *Sixty Sermons* lying around. Green might then have a new cancel title page printed, *A Sinner's Pathway to Heaven,* and try to palm off the *Sermons* as a new book just printed for himself. This issue also would have the collation:

A^4 (A1 is a cancel), $*^2$, and so on.

Often the cataloger will suspect that a leaf is a cancel but be unable to prove it. If, for instance, he had the Green issue, *Sinner's Pathway,* he would know from examination of the book that the title page (A1) or A4 had not been in the gathering as originally printed because their chain lines and watermark (if there were one) would not match. Cancellation of a title page is even today not unusual; so he would guess that A1, the title page, instead of A4, was a cancel particularly because the running title of the book was "Sixty Sermons" instead of "Sinner's Pathway." But it is also not unusual for a binder or book dealer to replace missing leaves in one copy of a book from another defective copy. So the cataloger could prove nothing unless he could compare his *Sinner's Pathway* with a copy of the *Sixty Sermons* (or with photostats or microfilm of it) or unless he could find a good printed bibliography in which the Founder's *Sermons* and its issues were thoroughly described. If he could find no proof, his collation of the *Pathway* could begin as follows:

A^4 (A1 and A4 are not conjugate), $*^2$, and so on.

He could then write a note below somewhat as follows:

Running title: "Sixty Sermons"; possibly A1, the title page, is a cancel.

In the same way he might have to describe the Blue issue:

A^4 (A1 and A4 are not conjugate), $*^2$, and so on;

and the Heggsby issue:

A^4, $*^2$, B^4 (B2 and B3 are not conjugate), C-2A^4, and so on.

Punctuation

Punctuation of a statement of collation depends largely upon common sense and personal preference, but it should be consistent. In the collations given above a comma sets off each unit, parentheses enclose parenthetical statements, and a period marks the close, just as these marks would be used in an ordinary sentence. Some catalogers may prefer to use punctuation marks more sparingly.

Collation of Real Books

The reader may think that life has been made unduly complex for the Founder's printer. Many books, it is true, do have collations which run as smoothly as

A-3B^4,

particularly modern books, which are generally entirely in type and are proofread by several people, including their authors, before printing begins at all. But just often enough to make his job challenging the cataloger will come across abnormal gatherings.

Insertions Again

Single-leaf additions are particularly common. Sir Thomas Elyot's folio dictionary, *Bibliotheca Eliotae* (London: T. Berthelet, 1548), for instance, has an unsigned leaf after L6; its text opens with the printed explanation that "all these wordes and phrases folowyng . . . shoulde haue come in before Caneo" on L6 verso. The gathering could be described:

L^8 (+ an unsigned leaf after L6).

Elkin Mathews took over Gordon Bottomley's *Gate of Smaragdus* (1904) from the Unicorn Press on the eve of publication, and at that time an extra leaf bearing the announcement of Mathews' publication of the book and a woodcut was tipped into the book between the preliminary blank leaf and the title page. An extra leaf bearing an engraved title appears after A1 in Bacon's *Historie of Life and Death* (London: Printed by I. Okes for H. Mosley, 1638); engraved titles or illustrations often occur on such added leaves in early books because engravings required more pressure than that normally given a form of type in the press.

John Brown's *Dissertation on . . . Poetry and Music* (London: Printed for L. Davis and C. Reymers, 1763), a 4to, has a final gathering 2I in which, as in 2B of the Founder's *Sermons,* leaves 1, 2, and 4 are conjugate with 6, 3, and 5, but only 1 and 2 are signed. The book's text ends, followed by the phrase "The End," on 1 verso; 2 and 3 contain an appendix with the pagination continued from 1 verso and with a catchword on 3 verso leading to the text of 4 recto; 4 recto and verso contains a poem followed on 4 verso by another "The End"; 5 has an advertisement; and 6 is blank. Probably the gathering originally consisted only of 1 and its conjugate blank, and 4 and 5 with more text and another "The End" were added later. The catchword on 3 verso is an indication that 2 and 3 were added last of all because it shows that when the printer set 3 verso, he knew the text of 4 recto. Perhaps the situation could best be described by an insertion formula like the second suggested for the *Sermons:*

> 2I^{6} (2I1, 2I2, and 2I4 are conjugate with 2I6, 2I3 and 2I5).

James Day's *New Spring of Divine Poetrie* (London: Printed by T. C. for H. Blunden, 1637), 4to, has the collation:

> A^{4} (+ a 2-leaf gathering signed (*) after A2), B-F^{4}, (F)^{4}, G^{2}.

Gathering (*) contains two commendatory poems like the Dean's distichs, and (F) contains additional poems by Day. Possibly (F) was not signed "H" and placed after G because G2 verso already had "Finis" printed at its foot.

George Lillo's *Works* (London: Printed for T. Davies, 1775) is a two-volume 8vo in eights. In volume one, however, after H2—a leaf that bears on its recto the secondary title of "The London merchant or . . . George Barnwell" —there is a dedication to Sir John Eyles, Bart., which occupies a four-leaf gathering with the first two leaves signed " *H3" and " *H4." This gathering and the final four-leaf gathering X of volume two (like the two small gatherings in the Founder's *Sermons*) were printed together as one sheet. "Directions to the Binder" are printed on X4v: "Take the half sheet of dedication here annexed (Signature *H3) and place it immediately before the prologue to George Barnwell." The collation statement for this book could be interrupted for the added gathering as in the first and second insertion formulas suggested for the *Sermons,* but it would also be like the third because at the end would come the parenthetical statement:

> (Part 1, gathering *H and part 2, gathering X were printed together as an 8-leaf sheet).

Such a note was not used with the *Sermons* because the cataloger could only suspect, but would have no way of knowing for sure, that the small gatherings had been printed together.

Division of a Sheet

Division of a sheet to form two small gatherings (as in the Founder's *Sermons*) is particularly common at the beginning or close of a book. A 4to collation such as

A^2, B-O^4, P^2

or an 8vo collation such as

A^4, B-O^8, P^4

or

A^2, B-O^8, P^6

or a 12mo collation such as

A^6, B-O^{12}, P^6

or

A^2, B-O^{12}, P^{10}

almost always means that the first and last gatherings have been printed together on one sheet and later cut apart. Sometimes the division is more complicated. *Psalmorum Davidis . . . Libri Quinque* (Londini: Typis T. Vautrollerij & impensis H. Francisci, 1580), an 8vo, has the collation:

¶^{6}, A-2T^8, 2V^{10}.

In this case 2V5 and 2V6 appear to have been printed as ¶1 and ¶8.

Sometimes, especially in the smaller formats, every sheet in the book is divided into two or more gatherings, apparently because gatherings with thick folds are hard for the binder to sew and cause the book to bulge at the spine. Thus books in 32mo or 16mo may consist entirely of gatherings of eight or even four leaves; books in 24mo or 12mo, twelve or six leaves; and books in 18mo, six leaves. Such books are especially common in the eighteenth century. Collation in such cases is simple enough.

Alternates

The cataloger will, however, come across books in 12mo by cutting with every twelve leaves forming two gatherings of eight and four leaves respectively instead of two gatherings of six leaves each. In such a case it is not necessary to name each gathering and tell how many leaves compose it. The collation of George Ruggle's *Ignoramus* (Editio septima; Dublinii, 1736), for instance, might be given simply:

A-O in alternate 8's and 4's.

Trollope's *Last Chronicle of Barset* (London: Smith, Elder & Co., 1867) is also gathered in alternate 8's and 4's. Occasionally there is even more subdivision. Sir John Vanbrugh's *Mistake* (Dublin: A. Rhames, 1726) has the collation:

A-K in alternate 4's and 2's.

Wrap-Arounds

A much more intriguing phenomenon is what (for want of a better term) may be called the "wrap-around" gathering. Dryden's *His Majesties Declaration Defended* (London: Printed for T. Davies, 1681), a folio, collates:

A^3, B-D^2, E^1.

At first one might guess that the book is incomplete with gatherings A and E each lacking one leaf. But no text is omitted, and in the Folger copy A1 and E1 are conjugate; E1 was printed as A4. If the leaves were still conjugate, the statement of collation might be followed by the parenthetical statement:

(E1 printed as A4; in this copy E1 and A1 are still conjugate.)

If they were no longer conjugate, it could be:

(Chain lines and watermark indicate that A1 and E1 probably were once conjugate.)

Bacon's *De Dignitate et Augmentis Scientiarum* (Parisiis: Typis P. Mettayer, 1624), a 4to, collates:

$*^2$, $2*^4$, $3*^2$, A-$3X^4$, $3Y^2$ (*1 and *2 are conjugate with 3*2 and 3*1).

Similar wrap-around gatherings with the affected leaves still conjugate in the Folger copies are in Nathaniel Lee's *Mithridates* (London: Printed by R. E. for J. Magnes and R. Bentley, 1678), John Caryll's *Naboth's Vinyard* (London: Printed for C. R., 1679), George Richards' *Essay on the Characteristic Differences between Ancient and Modern Poetry* [Oxford: 1789], and other books. Richard Ligon's *True & Exact History of . . . Barbadoes* (London: P. Parker and T. Guy, 1673) is a folio in two-leaf gatherings, but the two leaves of the final gathering 2I are not conjugate because 2I2 (so signed) was printed conjugate with the title page and 2I1 conjugate with an unsigned index leaf bearing at its foot a printed note to the binder: "Place this after folio 84"—i.e., between gatherings Y and Z. Apparently the wrap-around gathering was most used in the late seventeenth century and the eighteenth century.

Broadsheet Volumes

Stevenson remarks (p.cliv) that broadsheet volumes represent "a not uncommon format" for eighteenth- or nineteenth-century books with color plates, and he suggests (p.clx) a collation such as A-Z^1 for such books.

Cancels

Cancels are rather common. In Arthur Bedford's *Evil and Danger of Stage Plays* (Bristol: W. Bonny, 1706) B1 recto, on which the text begins, originally bore the caption title: "Hell upon earth: or, The language of the playhouse." But after the text had all been printed (B-P^8, Q^4, in 8vo), the title seems to have been changed (just as the printer had feared might happen to the Founder's *Sermons*). So the final leaf of the preliminary eight-leaf gathering A was printed to cancel B1 with the caption title changed to match the main title. The collation might be given:

A^7, B^8 (B1 is a cancel, printed as A8), C-P^8, Q^4.

In 1612 John Jaggard had his brother William print a

new 8vo edition of Bacon's *Essays* consisting of the original ten essays then current, with the collation:

A-G^8.

The text ended on G7 recto with G7 verso and G8 blank. But in that same year John Beale, apparently with Bacon's permission, got out a new collection of thirty-eight essays, including revised versions of nine of Jaggard's original ten. This put Jaggard on the spot; he might never be able to sell copies of his ten-essay collection still on his shelves. So he canceled G7 and G8 in his unsold copies and had his brother print additional gatherings

H-O^8

(just as we supposed the Founder's printer had added the extra sermon). On H1 recto the text of the canceled G7 recto was reprinted, and H1 verso-O8 recto contained Beale's extra twenty-nine essays. The collation of this issue might be written:

A-F^8, G^6, H-O^8 (Gatherings H-O cancel the original G7-G8).

The cancel title page which tries to palm off as a new book an old one which has not sold well (like the Founder's *Sinner's Pathway* title page which our Green foisted on the *Sixty Sermons*) is rather common. Thus Aelfric's *Saxon Treatise* (London: Printed by J. Haviland for H. Seile, 1623) was reissued as *Divers Ancient Monuments* (London: Printed by E. G. for F. Eglesfield, 1638); James Cleland's *ΗΡΩ-ΠΑΙΔΕΙΑ, or The Institution of a Young Noble Man* (Oxford: J. Barnes, 1607) became *The Scottish Academie, or, Institution of a Young Noble-Man* (London: Printed for E. White, 1611) and still later *The Instruction of a Young Noble-Man* (Oxford: J. Barnes, 1612); while Bacon's *Remaines* (London: Printed by B. Alsop for L. Chapman, 1648) was reissued as his *Mirrour of State and Eloquence* (London: Printed for L. Chapman, 1656) and his *De Dignitate et Augmentis Scientiarum* (Argentorati: Sumptibus J. J. Bockenhoferi, 1654) differs from the 1635 (Argentorati:

Sumptibus haeredum L. Zetzneri) edition only in that the entire first gathering is a cancel. In more recent times A. Conan Doyle's *Dreamland and Ghostland* (1887) was reissued as three separate books with cancel title pages calling Volumes 2 and 3 *Strange Stories of Coincidence* and *Ghost Stories and Presentiments,* respectively. Sometimes the publisher did not change the title but merely tried to stimulate sales, as when Trollope's *Macdermots of Ballycloran* (3 vols., 1847) was reissued in 1848 with cancel title pages describing the book as "an historical romance" and calling attention to the fact that Trollope was also the author of *The Kellys and the O'Kellys*.

The second issue with a cancel title page telling of different publishing arrangements (as when our Blue took over the *Sixty Sermons* from Black) often occurs—e.g., Bacon's *Essays* (London: Printed by J. Haviland for H. Barret and R. Whitaker, 1625—cancel: London: Printed by J. Haviland for H. Barret, 1625); John Lacy's *Sauny the Scot* (London: 1731—cancel: London: Printed for W. Feales, 1736).

A cancel often corrects an error or replaces something which might give offence, like the Founder's Hoggsty leaf. In the reprint of the British Museum *Catalogue* (Ann Arbor: J. W. Edwards, 1946) the leaf in Volume 20 which bore on its recto columns 189–90 ("Fuller" entries) had its verso printed with columns 191–92 from an earlier section ("Froelich" entries); and in Volume 54 the outer form of the gathering containing columns 5–36 ("Turkey"-"Turn" entries) was perfected by the inner form of an earlier gathering containing columns 93–124 ("Thym"-"Tiburtius" entries). The errors were discovered only after a number of copies had been sold, and correct cancel leaves and cancel gatherings were issued to purchasers. An elaborate series of cancels was introduced into the English edition of Somerset Maugham's *Painted Veil* (1925) substituting Tching-Yen for Hong-Kong as the scene of a part of the novel. In Theodore Dreiser's *Hoosier Holiday* (New York, 1916) one leaf (p.173–74) containing what might have been considered pro-German sentiment was canceled by a leaf with innocuous text. Sometimes leaves were simply canceled and not replaced. *The Annual Anthology* (Bristol and London: Printed by Biggs and Co. for T. N. Longman and O. Rees, 1799–1800), edited by Southey, normally lacks B8 (p.31–32) of Volume 1; the leaf contained Southey's "War Poem" and was canceled because of its unpatriotic sentiment (Kenneth Curry in B.S.A. *Papers* 42: 52 (1948).

Now and then a cancelland still may be found in a book along with the cancel. In the Folger collection, for instance, cancelland title pages may be found in copies of John Dryden's *Tyrannick Love* (London: Printed for H. Herringman, sold by R. Bently, J. Tonson, F. Saunders and T. Bennet, 1695), Robert Recorde's *Records Arithmetick* (London: Printed by M. F. for J. Harison, to be sold by N. Brooks, 1648) and Nathaniel Lee's *Mithridates* ([London]: Printed for R. Wellington and sold by F. Fawcet, 1702); and two cancelland leaves are in the first gathering of Joseph Ritson's *Quip Modest* (London: J. Johnson, 1788). A surviving cancelland does not create another issue because the cancelland is not really part of the book; it is there simply because someone forgot to remove it. It may be described in a parenthetical note following the entire collation—e.g., (In this copy the cancelland A2 survives). In at least one case a cancelland was left by intention. A line of type was omitted and other lines transposed on page 682 of *The Library of Congress Information Bulletin* for 7 November 1968. A separate corrected cancel leaf was prepared, but in order to avoid delay, the cancel was issued along with the uncorrected journal; a note stapled to it asked readers to substitute the corrected leaf themselves.

Unusual Signatures

One gathering in the Founder's *Sixty Sermons* was signed with an asterisk. In early books gatherings are rather often signed in unusual ways: with asterisks, stars, hands, crosses, two brackets, two parentheses, paragraph marks, plus signs, ampersands, question marks, leaves, one or two vertical lines, two or more dots or asterisks arranged to form a design, and so on. Probably the collation will be clearer if it reproduces such signatures instead of describing them—e.g.,

A^4, ☛^{4}, ¶^{2}, B-3Z^4.

is better than

A^4, hand^4, paragraph mark^4, B-3Z^4.

If the symbols appear in sequence, there is no need to reproduce them all. Thus, the collation of Thomas Cooper's *Nonae Novembris* (Oxoniae: Excudebat I. Barnesius, 1607), a 4to, would be expressed:

¶-3¶^{4}, A-P^4, Q^2.

rather than

¶^{4}, ¶¶^{4}, ¶¶¶^{4}, A-P^4, Q^2.

Sometimes combinations of two or more letters were used to sign only one gathering. Pseudo-Augustine's *Soliloquia* (Winterberg: J. Alacraw, 1484), a 4to, has the collation:

⟨abcd⟩^{8}, ⟨efgh⟩^{8}, ⟨iklm⟩^{8}, ⟨nop⟩^{6}.

Between the gatherings Ll and Oo in Nathaniel Bailey's *Universal Etymological English Dictionary* (London: Printed for R. Ware, J. and P. Knapton [etc.], 1749), an 8vo, is a gathering signed "Mm & Nn," and between gatherings T and Y in *Beauties of Shakespeare* (London: Printed for G. Kearsley, 1783), a 12mo, is a gathering signed "UX." Henry Fletcher's *Perfect Politician* (London: Printed for J. Crumpe, 1681), an 8vo, has a more complicated collation:

A^4, B-K^8, L^8 (signed L, L2, L3, L4, M, M2, M3, M4), N-T^8, U^4.

Occasionally a letter is omitted in a series of signatures. The anonymous anti-tobacco tract, *Work for Chimny-Sweepers* (London: Imprinted by T. Este for T. Bushell, 1602), a 4to, has the collation:

A-C^4, E-G^4.

This is because only the gatherings A-C were printed

by Este and E-G by Thomas Creede. Perhaps the two sections were printed at the same time and Creede expected Este to begin with B instead of A. The amalgamation of two letters for one signature also may result from such a printing division or (probably less frequently) from the cancellation of two gatherings by one.

In two of the books just noted U replaced V as a signature. This was not unusual after the distinction between U and V arose, and it requires no special notice in the statement of collation. But occasionally both U and V were used and sometimes, as in the Douai *Bible* (Doway: L. Kellam, 1609), W was included in a signature sequence. It is necessary to call attention to these extra letters in the collation statement:

A-U-Z^4.

or

A-W-Z^4.

A book signed with numerals is described in the same way as an alphabetical sequence:

1^4, 2-20^8, 21^4.

or

1-10 in alternate 8s and 4s.

Vowels alone are sometimes used as signatures; such a sequence, of course, cannot be condensed. Bacon's *Histoire de la Vie et de la Mort* (Paris: G. Loyson et J.-B. Loyson, 1647), an 8vo, collates:

ã^8, ẽ^8, A-2I^8.

Sometimes a gathering or series of gatherings is left unsigned. Probably one can describe such a situation most simply and clearly if he arbitrarily assigns a signature within brackets which will place it in proper sequence. Thus John Caryll's *Naboth's Vinyard* (London: Printed for C. R., 1679), a folio, would have the collation statement:

[A]^1, B-E^2, [F]^1 ([A]1 and [F]1 are conjugate).

Bacon's *Elements of the Common Lawes* (London: Printed by the assignes of J. More, to be sold by A. More, and H. Hood, 1636) a 4to, collates:

[A]^{4}, B-2A^{4}.

(but not

[A]-2A^{4},

because that would not make it clear that only the first gathering is unsigned), and Whittier's *In War Time and Other Poems* (1864):

[1-2]^{12}, 3-6^{12}, 7^{4}.

The word "unsigned" may be used instead of an arbitrary signature. This is readily understood; but "[F]^{1}" in the Caryll collation above would have to be called "another unsigned leaf" or "2d unsigned^{1}", and "[1-2]^{12}" in the third collation would require some such phrase as "two unsigned gatherings, 12 leaves each." This seems unnecessarily bunglesome. Moreover, it is conventional to enclose added material within brackets, and a reference in the notes to "[F]1" would locate the leaf at once with reference to other leaves in the books, whereas an "unsigned leaf" could be located only by referring to the collation statement. Consecutive unsigned gatherings do not require individual brackets; thus, it is "[1-2]^{12}" (*not* "[1]-[2]^{12}"). The "12" remains outside the brackets because it is true of the book regardless of how the gatherings may or may not be signed. Sometimes a book printed from plates may be imposed and gathered differently from the system indicated by the signatures. This may be shown by a collation such as:

[1-28]^{4} signed: 1-14^{8}.

or

[1-14]^{12}, [15]^{6} signed: [1]^{8}, 2-21^{8}, 22^{6}.

Some gatherings are actually signed by letters within parentheses or brackets; both are used in the fifth volume of the *Transactions* (Dublin: G. Bonham, 1795) of the Royal

Irish Academy. This can be explained in a parenthetical note immediately following the affected gatherings. Thus François Hédelin, abbé d'Aubignac's *Whole Art* (London: Printed for the author, and sold by W. Cadman, [etc.], 1684), a 4to, might be described:

A-S^4, [A]-[Y]^4 (actually so signed).

and Pierre Du Moulin's *Conference Held at Paris* (London: Printed for J. Barnes, 1615), a 4to:

A^2, (B)-(D)^4 (actually so signed).

If a leaf is wrongly signed, this may be stated within parentheses—e.g.,

A-C^4 (C2 signed C3), D-F^4.

Occasionally signatures or signature sequences are repeated in a book. Each repeated signature or series of signatures can be distinguished if given a series number within brackets. The collations would then appear as:

A^4, [2d] A-G^4, [3d] A-H^4.

and

A-G^4, [2d] A-G^4, [3d] A-C^4, [4th] A-F^4.

Actually the G after the second A is itself also a second, the C after the third A is also a third, and the F after the fourth A is a third F. But these are pedantic and obvious distinctions whose observance would only clutter the description. Frequently a repeated signature sequence marks the beginning of a new part, or even a new volume, of the work. In such a case the two collation statements above could be simply:

Part 1: A^4, [2d] A-G^4; Part 2: A-H^4.

and

Part 1: A-G^4; Part 2: A-G^4; Part 3: A-C^4; Part 4: A-F^4.

Bacon's *Sylva Sylvarum* (London: Printed for W. Lee, sold by T. Williams and W. Place, 1658), a folio, has the collation:

[A]^2, A^4 (A1 is a cancel), (a)^4, B-R^6 (R3 signed E3), S-T^6, V-Y^4, a^4 (a2 signed A2), b-e^4 (e1 signed E), [2d] A-B^2, [2d] C-K^4.

In Willem Sewel's *History of the . . . Quakers* (3d ed., cor. Philadelphia: S. Keimer, 1728), gathering Zzzzz is followed by a second Aaaaa; apparently the interruption marks the point at which Franklin and Meredith began printing the book.

Full-Page Illustrations

Full-page engravings, woodcuts, or other illustrations are not abundant in ordinary books. Often, particularly if they are engravings, they are not conjugate with other leaves. Sometimes they are in a numbered sequence which may be indicated in the table of contents or in a printed instruction for the binder.

Full-page illustrations should be included in the statement of collation by gatherings only if they are actually conjugate with other leaves; if they are on disjunct leaves scattered throughout the book, they will result in a series of annoying one-leaf interruptions in the statement. They may be noted separately after the collation—e.g., "front." or "15 engraved plates." If any illustration is lacking or obviously misbound, this should be noted. Stevenson has some interesting suggestions about the description of books largely made up of plates.

Odd and Even Numbers

When a binder sews a gathering through the fold, he fastens with one thread every pair of conjugate leaves in the gathering. But a single leaf can be sewed only if there is a stub provided in place of its conjugate leaf; otherwise it must be pasted in. Either solution causes the binder extra work, and a single leaf may come loose and be lost more easily than one of a pair of conjugate leaves. For this reason a gathering normally has an even number of leaves. In a statement of collation it is generally safe to assume that if a gathering has an odd number of leaves, one or more leaves have been lost. Chain lines, watermarks, and the sewing thread at the center fold will usually tell how large the gathering originally was and which leaves are missing.

A few gatherings, however, were issued with an odd number of leaves. If the cause was a cancel, an insertion, or a wrap-around, the chain lines and watermarks again tell, or at least suggest, the story in most books printed prior to 1800. But sometimes a leaf was canceled and not replaced (as in the *Annual Anthology;* see above, p.85); or it may have been printed for use in another book. On the last leaf of Dryden's *Secret Love* (London: Printed for H. Herringman, to be sold by R. Bentley, 1691), for instance, was printed the title of *The Works of Mr. Thomas Otway* (London: Printed for R. Bentley, 1691). One can never be sure a missing leaf actually has been lost unless he knows a duplicate copy of the book contains it. Otherwise the leaf may have been canceled, or it may have been used in another book for which it was printed and therefore does not really belong with the book in hand at all. Such leaves are rare, and it is not a seriously misleading error to describe them as simply lacking. But if there is evidence that the book was issued with a leaf or leaves canceled, the collation should reflect the publisher's intention:

A-G^4, H^3 (H4 canceled).

Imperfections

A cataloger's statement of collation does not describe a particular copy of a book; instead (as in ordinary cataloging), it describes an ideally complete copy with all leaves in proper sequence, just as they were when the book was first issued. For this reason imperfections in the copy being cataloged are not (like cancels, for instance) noted immediately after the affected gathering but come, instead, at the close of the entire collation by gatherings, thus:

A-$3B^4$ (A1 lacking).

or

A-3B⁴ (A1 [title leaf] lacking).

or

A-3B⁴ (duplicate gathering B bound in).

A duplicate gathering bound in a book does not create a special issue of that book, because the survival of the duplicate gathering, like the survival of a cancelland, is merely a binder's error. A surviving cancelland might be described:

A-3B⁴ (G1 is a cancel; in this copy the cancelland also survives).

A made-up copy might be described:

A-3B⁴ (gatherings 2G and 3A lacking, replaced by gatherings from another copy).

A bibliographer will, presumably, have examined all copies of the book; he will, therefore, know in every case what the ideal copy should be like. A cataloger, however, is limited to such information as he may find in printed catalogs and bibliographies; he may not find a description of an ideal copy, and his collation may end up something like this:

A-2Z⁴ (all after gathering 2Z lacking).

misbound leaves or gatherings are not uncommon:

A-3B⁴ (gathering C misbound after D4).

This list of kinds of imperfections does not pretend to be complete. For any imperfection all that is needed is a brief, simple statement of the problem.

Format, Size, and Type

Immediately following or immediately preceding the collation by gatherings should come a statement of format—e.g., 4to. Also the size of the page may be added along with the note that the leaves have (or have not) been trimmed, or are still uncut. For early books the cataloger may add the kind of type (black letter, roman, or italic) and the size of the space occupied by type on a specific page. But notes of size and type are needed only if the cataloger knows that these features are the distinctive differences between the book in hand and other copies, editions, or issues of the book; otherwise, the principle of calculated risk applies.

Pagination

Equally important with collation by gatherings is collation by pages. This will account for every page, whether blank or not, included in the collation by gatherings. Indicate only the last page number in each sequence. The collation by gatherings of the Founder's *Sermons* (see p.74) was:

A^4, *^{2}, B-2A^4, 2B^4 (+a 2-leaf unsigned gathering after 2B3), 2C-3B^4.

The pagination statement might be:

[12], 194, 191-374, [2].

The twelve unnumbered pages occupy the preliminary gatherings A and *; if the printer had given them roman numerals, the statement would open:

xii, 194, etc.

The text itself began on B1 recto, which was numbered page 1, and pagination sequence continued unbroken, except for errors, through 2B3 verso (p.190). Here the two-leaf unsigned gathering was inserted. If the printer assigned numbers 191–94 to its pages, this would result in the statement as given above. If he assigned no page numbers to the inserted leaves, the pagination statement would run:

[12], 190, [4], 191-374, [2].

There would be, no doubt, misnumbered pages, and it might be a help in some cases to list them. The various issues of the Founder's book, for instance, would have the same pagination errors (unless, of course, the printer had corrected some of them while the book was going through the press); a note of these errors would help the reader of the card for one issue to suspect that it was an issue (rather than an edition) even before he might have seen either book. But he would already have been alerted by the statements of collation and pagination, and in any event he would have to see the books himself before he could determine their relationship to his own satisfaction. It is, in short, a good calculated risk to omit mention of pagination errors. The same is true of unnumbered pages in a pagination sequence. If, for instance, B1 recto (p.1) had been unnumbered, this fact need not have been noted.

Collation: Cataloger and Bibliographer

Using the suggestions of McKerrow and especially Greg, Bowers has developed a collation formula which he calls "shorthand" as opposed to the "longhand" collation which he supposes catalogers use. Probably no cataloger will want to use shorthand collation, at least completely, because it employs some arbitrary symbols which might not be understood by the ordinary user of a library catalog. On the other hand, a cataloger will need to consult printed bibliographies containing shorthand descriptions of copies of the book he is cataloging. The following notes, based on Bowers (p.28–30 and 457–62), may be of some help toward understanding such descriptions.

In order to show what he thinks are the advantages of shorthand collation, Bowers constructs two statements of collation and a note of reference to each. The following is what he imagines might be written by someone unacquainted with his formula:

Collation—4^0: [ ]^4 A^4 (A4 is a cancel)-H^4 [ ]^2 I-X^4 Y^3 (Y4 missing, used to print cancel leaf A4).

Reference—The title page on [ ] 1 of the preliminary gathering is identical, except for the imprint, with that on [ ] 1 following gathering H; cancel A4 contains a longer errata list than the errata list on the original A4 leaf. The errata on cancel A4 include readings from signatures B through X, whereas the list on the original A4 was confined to signatures B through H.

What Bowers calls "a true formulary collation" and its note of reference follow:

Collation—4^0: π^4 A^4 ($\pm$ A4 [= Y4]) B-H^4 χ^2 I-X^4 Y^4 (-Y4).

Reference—The title page on π1 is identical except for the imprint with that on $^H\chi$1; leaf A(A4) contains a longer errata list than did A4; the errata on A(A4) include readings from B-X, whereas the list on A4 was confined to B-H.

Bowers remarks that "the advantage of this compact formula over the loquacious and interrupted formula of the longhand writer is worth something, but of more value is the ease and clarity of reference" (p.29). Earlier he had urged "the necessity to reduce as much description as possible to formulas, since concision is usually of the utmost importance" (p.26).

Bowers' shorthand formula is, indeed, compact enough, but his reference to it may be condensed to read:

The title on π1 is identical except for imprint with that on $^H\chi$1; A(A4) errata list applies to B-X, that on A4 applied only to B-H.

So, although "ease and clarity of reference" are the major benefits of shorthand collation, concision of reference itself appears not to be "of the utmost importance." The road to concision is not always paved with shorthand formula symbols only.

Suppose we now return to the statement of collation and note of reference which Bowers imagines might be written by someone unacquainted with his shorthand formula. Bowers properly calls these statements "loquacious." Reconstructed by a system such as I have suggested above, they might read somewhat as follows:

Collation—4^0: $[A]^4$ A^4 (A4 is a cancel) B-H^4 $[I]^2$ I-X^4Y^3 (Y4 used to print cancel A4).

Reference—The title on [A]1 is identical except for imprint with that on [I]1. Cancel A4 errata list applies to B-X; that on original A4 applied only to B-H.

If these imagined statements are any indication, a Bowers

shorthand statement of collation might be about half as long as a statement of collation such as I have suggested. The space saved on a catalog card would not be great—frequently no more than one line per book—and the shorthand symbols would, indeed, be Greek to the catalog user. A printed bibliography, of course, can carry a list of symbols in the preface to which a reader may turn, albeit with some muttering, for enlightenment. On the other hand, a Bowers statement of reference would require more space than such a reference as I have suggested.

The meaning of the Bowers shorthand symbols used in his collation statement given above is clear from the context. A list of other ingenious symbols and devices used by Bowers follows, accompanied in a parallel column by simpler statements which might be more readily understood by catalog users:

BOWERS STATEMENT	SIMPLER STATEMENT
Duplicated signatures	
A-S^4, ^{2}A-X^4	A-S^4 [2d] A-X^4
Inferred signatures	
[A]^4 B-C^4 or *A*^{4} B-C^4	[A]^4 B-C^4
but	and
π^2 A-Y^4	[A]^2 A-Y^4
π-2π^4 A-P^4	[A-B]^4 A-P^4
A-C^4 χ^2 D-F^4	A-C^4 [D]^2 D-F^4
but	
A-C^4 *D*^{2} E-F^4	A-C^4 [D]^2 E-F^4
Inserted disjunct leaves	
A-C^4 D^4 (D4 + D5)	A-D^4 (+ a leaf signed D5 after D4)
A-F^4 G^4 (G4 + 'G5', G6)	A-G^4 (+2 disjunct leaves after G4, the first signed G5)
A-I^4 K^4 (K3 + 'K4')	A-K^4 (+ a leaf signed K4 after K3)
A-M^4 N^4 (N2 + χ1)	A-N^4 (+ an unsigned leaf after N2)
A-R^{4}S^4 (S2 + ¶S2)	A-S^4 (+ a leaf signed ¶S2 after S2)
A-S^4 T^4 (T3 + 'T4', χ1)	A-T^4 (+2 disjunct leaves after T3, the first signed T4)

Inserted folds

A-D^4 E^4 (E4 + *E5.6)	A-E^4(+2 conjugate leaves after E4, the first signed *E5)
A-E^4 F^4 (F1 + ¶^{2})	A-F^4 (+ a two-leaf gathering signed ¶ after F1)
A-G^{4}H^4 (H2 + χ^2)	A-H^4 (+ an unsigned 2-leaf gathering after H2)

Cancellation

A-C^{4}D^4 (−D1)	A-C^{4}D^3 (D1 canceled)
A-G^{4}H4 (−H1.4)	A-G^{4}H^2 (original H1 and H4 canceled)
A-L^{4}M^4 (−M3,4)	A-L^{4}M^2 (M3 and M4 canceled)
A-G^{4}H^4 (−H1.4 + H1,4)	A-H^4 (H1 and H4, disjunct leaves, are cancels)
A-C^{4}D^4 (−D1 + *D1)	A-D^4 (D1 is a cancel signed *D1)
A^{4}B^4 (−B3 + 'B3'.1)	A-B^4 (B3 canceled by a 2-leaf gathering with 1st leaf signed B3)
A-B^{4}C^4 (−C2 + χ^2)	A-B^4,C^5 (original C2 canceled by unsigned 2-leaf gathering)
A-C^{4}D^4 (−D2.3 + χ1)	A-C^{4}D^3 (D2, unsigned, cancels D2 and D3)

A few of Bowers' reference devices may be noted: "A(o)" means the outer form of gathering A and "A(i)" the inner form. "A-F(o)" means the outer forms of gatherings A-F; "A-F(i)" the inner forms. The symbol "$" may apply to all the gatherings in a book or all except for a few. If all four leaves of every gathering in a quarto were signed, one could write: "$4 signed." If the first six leaves of every gathering except for gatherings C, H, and M were signed, one could write: "$6(−CHM6) signed."

Collation: Summary

So the physical makeup of the book may be set forth in a statement of collation which tells: (1) how many gatherings there are in the book and how many leaves there are in each gathering, and (2) how many pages there are in the entire book. A statement of collation is most useful when its language is simple and direct and free of jargon.

7. The Rest of the Job

When a cataloger has transcribed a title and given collation by gatherings and by pagination, he has done much to set that book apart from all others. How much more is necessary?

Contents

It is fashionable in some printed bibliographies and on some catalog cards to have an elaborate statement of contents. Such a statement, like the pagination, accounts for every page included in the collation by gatherings with mention, and perhaps some transcription, of separate title pages. But generally such a statement is not necessary to identify the book. If the contents include more (or less) than the book's title indicates, or if something special has happened to some portion of the book—e.g., if it was also published separately—this can be stated in a brief note.

Text

The text of the book may be printed in some unusual way. Every page, for instance, may be within decorative borders, or illustrations may be included in the text, or the text may be in two or more columns. If the running title of the text differs greatly from the title-page title, this should be noted because, as with the Founder's *Sermons* and *Sinner's Pathway,* this may betray a great deal about the history of the book's printing. But generally notes of whatever seems unusual in the printing of the text may be omitted.

Slip Cancels

When the Founder caught the Heggsby-Hoggsty error, the printer might have corrected the sheets already printed by printing little slips of paper with "Heggsby" on them and then pasting these slips over the offending "Hoggsty." Such a slip is generally called a "slip cancel," and, although it must have been a nuisance to hunt up the proper page and paste the slip in where it belonged in each copy, it did save the trouble of resetting, printing, and inserting an entire cancel leaf. Slip cancels are rather common in early books, and sometimes they appear in modern books. W. C. Firebaugh's *The Inns of the Middle Ages* (Chicago: Pascal Covici, 1924), for instance, was reissued with a slip cancel imprint: "London, Grant Richards Ltd. . . . 1925." Probably the cataloger will pass over many slip cancels because he does not have time to look carefully for them. But when he does come across one, it is worthwhile to call attention to it in a brief note.

Bindings

A leather binding is not often significant. It is seldom contemporary, and with a book printed prior to 1800 it would be quite difficult to prove that even a contemporary binding was put on by the bookseller and that all copies of the book were issued in identical bindings. Generally only an expert can tell with certainty the age and kind of leather in a binding. If the binder has signed his work, the cataloger will, of course, record that fact.

In the latter half of the eighteenth century publishers began to issue books in gray or blue paper boards with or without paper labels on the spine. Beginning with the 1820s these paper boards gave way to cloth (and later half-cloth) bindings, and in the 1830s lettering directly on the cloth began to replace the printed paper labels. Many of the paper boards and most cloth bindings are publisher's bindings; that is, they are integral parts of the books as issued originally. For this reason the description of such books as physical objects would logically include the binding and the binder's title. The cloth may be described in everyday language, and the title transcription may follow the rules for transcription of the title page.

Condition and History

The condition of the book may be briefly noted if it affects the text—e.g.:

Wormholes.
Part of C2 torn away slightly affecting text.
Closely trimmed affecting headlines and marginal notes.

The history of the book may be important if a noted former owner is involved. Seymour de Ricci's *English Collectors of Books & Manuscripts* (Cambridge Univ. Pr., 1930) and Carl L. Cannon's *American Book Collectors and Collecting* (New York: Wilson, 1941) tell of the more prominent British and American owners of books and how to identify their marks of ownership. Books such as Edwin Wolf 2nd and John F. Fleming's *Rosenbach, A Biography* (Cleveland and New York: World, 1960) help to bring this knowledge up to date.

Duplicates

Probably there is no such thing as a duplicate of an early book printed on the handpress. Gatherings otherwise identical in two copies may have different watermarks and different combinations of errors and press corrections (cf. the Hoggsty-Heggsby versions of the Founder's book) and the books themselves may have different combinations of variant gatherings. But unless there is more than this sort of difference, for all practical purposes the two books are duplicates.

The cataloger can be sure there are no further differences only if he checks every word on every page of each copy; this can be done mechanically by the bibliographer if he has a machine called the Hinman collator, but the cataloger has time to check carefully only a few points. If the collation and pagination of two copies are identical, what of the errors in catchwords, signatures, and page numbers? (Of course, a corrected error may only be the result of correction while printing.) Pick three or more pages at random and check the type. Do the same breaks in letters, the same unusual spaces between words, the same spelling, the same errors, the same kinds of type appear on these pages in both copies? Do the signatures checked at random have the same words in the same place in the text above them? If there are press numbers, are they the same in both copies and do they, like the signatures, have the same relation to the text directly above them?

It may well be that some day a bibliographer will come along and find a major difference in other parts of the book, but the cataloger does not have his kind of time. If he has done the checking correctly, he can only apply again the principle of calculated risk. In a note he can describe the second book as apparently another copy and indicate such minor variations as he may have found—e.g., a corrected page number.

Special Cataloging Practices

Most rare books are kept in closed stacks; this removes any reason for subject classification. Instead, special kinds of grouping may be more useful. A large number of copies of books listed in a particular bibliography may be shelved together in the sequence of the bibliography. All the books in a particular language may be shelved alphabetically by author. Sometimes it is helpful to keep together books in a private collection which the library has bought or received by gift. Special format or other characteristics may require grouping—e.g., all playbills, all promptbooks, all extra-illustrated books, etc.

Special catalog files may be useful—e.g., chronological files for earlier books, indexes of printers and publishers, catalogs of former owners.

The Conclusion of the Whole Matter

A cataloger can catalog almost any rare book adequately if he has an intelligent skepticism. The important thing is not so much what he does to the card as what he does to the book.

He will examine the book as a physical entity, and as he does so, he will keep asking three questions: (1) Is everything what it seems or professes to be? (2) What features are significant? (3) Is the book complete?

Then, briefly and clearly, he will tell of the chief ways in which that book may differ from other editions and issues of that particular title and all other copies of that particular edition and issue. This means that he will give: (1) rather brief title and imprint; (2) collation by gatherings in simple language; (3) collation by pages; and (4) other descriptive notes as necessary. He will be thorough and accurate, but he will not try to tell everything. Only if he takes the calculated risk of leaving out much will he have time to get the job done.

Index